PICNICS

JOAN
CHATFIELD-
TAYLOR

PUBLISHED BY TAYLOR & NG · SAN FRANCISCO · 1980

TO
PHILIPPE,
CHRISTINA,
& MATTHEW

ISBN 0-912738-13-8

Library of Congress Card No. 79-64872
Printed in the United States of America
Copyright © 1980 Joan Chatfield-Taylor
Published by Taylor & Ng
P.O. Box 200
Brisbane, California 94005
    All Rights Reserved
    First Edition First Printing 1980
Distributed by Random House, Inc.
and in Canada by Random House of Canada, Ltd.
ISBN 0-394-73760-1

Photography by Andrew J. Cohen

PICNICS

Joan Chatfield-Taylor is a feature writer for the San Francisco Chronicle. Her interest in food and travel has led her to cook in the styles of many countries. Her fondness for the vivid, flavorful food of the countries around the Mediterranean was especially useful in preparing this book of exciting recipes for warm-weather meals outdoors. She lives in San Francisco with her husband and their two children.

For suggestions and recipes willingly shared, I want to thank Elinor Chatfield-Taylor, Yvonne Henry, Wendell Thomas, Marian Lever, Sally Culley, Maria Quinn, Joanna Thompson, Angie Thieriot, and Merces Freemon.

TABLE OF CONTENTS

IN PRAISE OF PICNICS

History does not record the first person who chose to eat outside even though he had a perfectly good dining room at hand. This imaginative soul deserves credit as the originator of the picnic; he—or she—was a Pied Piper who led us all outdoors with our baskets, our salami and our cheese to let nature enhance the ordinary act of eating.

The picnic is more than just a meal. It is a festive occasion. Webster's first definition of the word "picnic" emphasizes the communal nature of the event; a picnic is "a social entertainment at which each person contributes food to a common table."

In the second definition the dictionary gets around to the other key element: a picnic is "an excursion or an outing . . . in the open." It is no less of a picnic if you eat in your own backyard, but there is a greater sense of achievement found in packing up the meal in baskets and bottles, then laying out a splendid feast in the improbable setting of a meadow or a beach.

Thirdly, a picnic is a break from ordinary routine. In its broadest sense, quite apart from eating, the dictionary defines a picnic as "a pleasant or amusing experience:

a time free of ordinary cares or responsibilities."

As more of us live out our lives in cities, a picnic becomes increasingly special. An outdoor meal is a luxury, a little victory over everyday urban life. Even in a miniscule, manicured city garden, it is a pleasant contact with natural phenomena that are often airconditioned away beyond windows that don't open.

It is not always perfectly comfortable. Outdoor meals are subject to the vagaries of climate, from scorching sun to chilly breezes. Poison oak and ants create problems unknown in the average dining room. Sitting on the ground is not necessarily as easy as sitting in an armchair.

I still love to eat outdoors. Outdoor meals, whether luxurious or Spartan, remain etched on my memory more vividly than many elaborate indoor feasts. I remember every detail of a picnic on the Greek island of Corfu, with the grass soft under the olive trees, the Adriatic lapping politely at a spit of sand a few yards away, and a flock of sheep, complete with bells, wandering by. The menu included freshly-caught lobster and tiny strawberries sold in baskets by children along the

road. I remember, too, a lunch in a rocky field high in the Atlas mountains of Morocco, where there was nothing but stones, blue sky and silence. Canned tuna, a loaf of bread and warmish mineral water were the sum total of the menu.

The first picnic was luxurious, the second was not, but both were unforgettable.

At its best, the outdoor meal is a giant step away from the routine of every day. It deserves special food to make it even more extraordinary.

Exceptional Food— To Go

Is there a difference between ordinary food and outdoor food? There should be, to underline the fact that a picnic isn't a routine event.

In choosing recipes for this book, I tried to think of food better suited to outdoor consumption than to indoor meals. There is nothing to stop anyone from eating a meat loaf sandwich at the dining room table, but it seems like outdoor food. You can carefully transport a molded fish mousse gilded with mayonnaise and cucumber slices to a country field, but it seems like

1

a showy tour de force, contrary to the whole point of eating outside.

Picnic food should be simple food. It is earthy food and it is healthy food, with all the natural flavors in the open. It should be vividly flavored and simply prepared. It is an opportunity to take advantage of fresh fruits and vegetables.

Picnic food should be easy to eat, even when you are perched on a rock or sitting cross-legged on the beach. The best outdoor food needs no last-minute cooking, unless a barbecue is part of the festivities. Although a few of the recipes in this book involve planning ahead to the extent of cooking the night before, most of them are designed to be made and assembled the morning of the meal. You will be able to eat in style, even if the outdoor meal is a last-minute project.

Same-day cooking often eliminates having to put the food in the refrigerator. This may sound like heresy to Americans who regard their vast and gleaming refrigerators as a Maginot line between themselves and disease, but refrigeration is one of the worst things that can happen to the taste of food. It dries out meats, and it kills the delicate tastes of salads and vegetables. Instead, put the finished dishes in a cool place, letting the flavors meld together for a couple of hours. If you must refrigerate a

dish, give it time to return to room temperature before it is served.

There are exceptions. Although most salads, vegetables, fruits and cooked meats are fine to eat if they have been left unchilled for several hours, dishes involving eggs are less accommodating in hot weather. Raw eggs are particularly vulnerable to heat, which is one reason this book provides alternatives to mayonnaise. Cooked eggs are less dangerous; a quiche can be left in a cool place for a couple of hours without risk.

Other foods taste better if they're icy cold. Recipes involving gelatin are not designed to travel far from the shelter of an effective ice chest or a refrigerator. Cold soups taste better the colder they are. Fruit salads stay crisper and fresher if they are kept cold.

A Few Tricks

There are some tricks to cooking food that will be eaten cool or cold. As the food cools, seasonings sometimes change in intensity. Raw garlic and hot chili peppers tend to become more intense as they permeate the food; to keep this under control, it is often better to use a whole, peeled, lightly-crushed clove of garlic or a whole chili pepper to flavor a cold dish. As soon as the dish is sufficiently flavored, the garlic or the pepper can be removed.

Salt, on the other hand, tends to fade away as the food gets colder. You can use as much as twice the normal amount of salt when you are cooking food that will be served cold. Be prepared to taste for salt after the dish has cooled.

Even if you prefer the delicate taste of peanut oil for salads indoors, outdoor food seems to demand the more definite taste of olive oil. I use a pale green California oil with a heavy, fruity taste for everything except mayonnaise, where I still prefer peanut oil. Tastes vary, and you should try using different oils.

Yogurt is an excellent substitute for cream or sour cream when you're planning to travel outdoors with the meal. It's less caloric, and it doesn't spoil. Try it in cold soups, and use it to lighten and stabilize mayonnaise.

There is no substitute, on the other hand, for fresh herbs. If the herb is not going to be cooked, it is better to substitute one fresh herb for another if you can't get the one specified in the recipe. If the herb will be cooked, you can substitute dried herbs, using one-third to one-half the amount of fresh.

Getting There Is Half The Battle

Picnics seem like less of an effort once you have assembled the perfect basket, containers, ground cover, plates, cutlery and glasses. The only trouble is that there's no agreement on what the perfect items are.

We happen to swear by a classic English picnic basket, the kind with the plates and cutlery neatly strapped into place. Other picnickers use big square baskets, open on top to let the wine and the French bread stick out. Others like canvas sailing bags, and then there are the rugged types who won't take anything that doesn't fit into a backpack.

Whatever you choose, small, un-bulky receptacles are preferable to massive chests and baskets. It's easier to ask the children to carry a loaf of bread or a jug of wine than to struggle with an enormous chest that weighs 100 pounds filled.

Inside our basket we have a hodgepodge of containers, starting with the rectangular metal boxes that came with it. They were originally intended for meticulously-trimmed sandwiches in wax paper—wrapped by the butler, perhaps. I don't provide such decorous fare, but the sandwich boxes are handy containers for soft fruit, bunches of radishes, a pepper grinder, salt shaker, tubes of mustard and other small items that would otherwise drift to the bottom of the basket.

The best food containers I've seen are rectangular clear plastic boxes made by a Dutch company called Rosti. Many department stores and specialty kitchenware stores now carry them. Their tight-fitting lids make them airtight and waterproof, so they are ideal as storage containers on boats as well as for picnics. They're rectangular and waste less space in a right-angled basket than do round containers.

One good knife, strong enough to slice French bread and cold meats, is laid blade-down along the side of the basket. We also carry a Swiss army knife, the kind that has a corkscrew, several blades, a bottle opener and a can opener. A lightweight cutting board that doubles as a serving platter is another essential. A Thermos bottle and napkins are kept permanently in the basket.

For keeping things cool, inexpensive Styrofoam containers and ice substitutes frozen beforehand are simple items that have worked for us, even in the desert.

More important than the equipment itself is having it ready the moment someone feels like a picnic. The sharp knife, the salt shaker and the corkscrew kept permanently in the basket will save you from all those recriminations that start out, "Who forgot the. . .?"

Serves Six

Officially, the recipes in this book are planned to serve six, assuming that they are served as part of a menu of two or three different dishes, plus dessert. Unofficially, given the communal nature of most picnics, with many people bringing and sharing several different dishes, they will probably stretch much further.

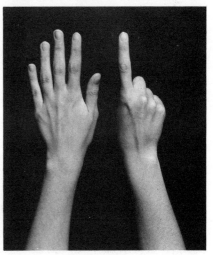

SOUP OF THE DAY

Cold soups are a civilized beginning to any outdoor meal. They're easy to make and easy to transport in a pre-chilled Thermos bottle. The simplest way to serve them is in plastic cups, with or without spoons.

One word of warning. If you make your own chicken stock, be careful about using it in these soups. Some homemade stocks are so filled with natural gelatin that they gel firmly when chilled and thicken your soup more than you intended. Either use canned broth or dilute your own stock enough with water, cream, milk or another appropriate liquid so that it won't solidify the finished soup.

Cold soups should always be served really cold. Give them several hours in the refrigerator, and then be sure to taste for seasoning before you serve them. Chances are that the soup will need more salt.

Curried Cream of Zucchini Soup

8 small zucchini, scrubbed and trimmed but not peeled
1 cup onion, chopped
1 clove garlic, chopped
3 cups chicken stock
1 teaspoon curry powder
1 cup milk
½ cup heavy cream
1 teaspoon salt
white pepper
½ cup sour cream or yogurt
¼ cup parsley or chives, finely chopped

Cut zucchini horizontally into one-inch slices. In a saucepan, simmer the zucchini with stock, onion, garlic and curry powder. Remove from heat and puree in a blender, food processor or food mill. Add milk and cream, and season with salt and pepper. Chill for several hours. Check the seasoning, and serve with a tablespoon of sour cream or yogurt and a sprinkling of chopped fresh parsley or chives.

Jellied Consomme with Fresh Herbs

1 ten-ounce can of chicken
    consomme
1 ten-ounce can of beef
    consomme
1 ten-ounce can of water
2 tomatoes, peeled, seeded and
    coarsely chopped
½ cup fresh herbs, such as tarra-
    gon, chives and parsley,
    minced very fine
1 tablespoon gelatin
⅓ cup Madeira
½ cup sour cream

Simmer soups, water and tomatoes together for 15 minutes.
Dissolve gelatin in Madeira. Remove soup from heat, cool for a
few minutes, and stir in gelatin
and herbs. Chill in the refrigerator
until the soup is well-gelled. Serve
with a spoonful of sour cream on
each serving.

Cucumber Soup

This is a particularly cooling soup
with a Middle Eastern flavor.

1 large English cucumber or 2
    regular cucumbers
2 tablespoons scallions, finely-
    chopped
1 cup chicken broth
2 cups plain yogurt
3 tablespoons fresh mint,
    chopped
1 teaspoon salt
white pepper

Peel cucumbers, halve them
lengthwise and remove the seeds
with a spoon. In a blender or food
processor, puree them with scallions. Add chicken broth, yogurt,
salt and pepper. Stir in mint, and
chill the soup for several hours before serving.

Egg and Lemon Soup

The Greek egg and lemon soup
called avgolomeno is usually
served hot, but it is also delicious
cold.

⅓ cup lemon juice
3 cups chicken broth
1 cup heavy cream
4 egg yolks
1 cup cooked rice
1 teaspoon salt
white pepper

In a heavy two-quart saucepan,
heat chicken broth and lemon
juice to a simmer. Beat egg yolks
and cream together in a small
bowl. Stir ½ cup of the broth into
the egg and cream mixture. Then
pour eggs and cream in a thin
stream into the saucepan of
broth, stirring frequently over
medium-low heat until it thickens
slightly. Add salt, pepper and rice.
Chill for several hours.

Cold Pea Soup With Mint

2 cups shelled peas (or 2 pack-
    ages frozen peas)
3 lettuce leaves
½ cup shallots or green onions,
    chopped
¼ cup heavy cream
4 cups chicken stock
¾ cup plain yogurt
3 tablespoons fresh mint,
    chopped
1 teaspoon salt

Simmer peas, lettuce, onions or
shallots and cream for about ten
minutes in a covered saucepan.
Add chicken stock and simmer for
another five minutes. Puree in a
blender, food processor or food
mill. Pour the soup through a
sieve, and cool before adding
yogurt, salt and two tablespoons
mint. Chill for several hours and
garnish with the remaining mint.

Vichyssoise

This soup reminds me of my grandmother, who used to take me to lunch in her New York hotel in the summer. Inevitably, the meal started with a cup of vichyssoise, icy cold in a bed of ice and sprinkled with chives. Since then, vichyssoise has dropped from fashion as the favorite summer soup. It doesn't deserve its oblivion, since the combination of leeks and potatoes and cream is as good as ever, and blenders and food processors have made it easy to make.

2 cups potatoes, peeled and
　　sliced
2 cups leeks (or a combination of
　　leeks and onions), sliced
4 cups chicken broth
½ cup chives, chopped
1 cup cream, sour cream, or
　　yogurt; or a combination of
　　half cream, and half sour
　　cream or yogurt
1 teaspoon salt

Simmer leeks and potatoes in chicken broth until the potatoes are tender. Puree them in a blender or food processor, or put them through a food mill. Cool, then add most of the chives, salt and the cream, sour cream, or yogurt. Chill for several hours, and serve garnished with the remaining chives.

Sorrel Soup

The bitter taste of sorrel, one of the easiest leaf greens to grow, results in a soup that is delicious hot, even better cold.

2 cups sorrel leaves, stemmed
　　and cut in narrow strips
3 tablespoons butter
1 quart rich chicken broth
3 egg yolks
1 cup heavy cream
1 teaspoon salt
pepper

Melt butter in a large, heavy saucepan. Add sorrel and stir for a few minutes over medium heat until it is wilted. Add chicken stock and simmer, covered, for 20 minutes. Beat egg yolks and heavy cream together. Add a few spoonfuls of hot liquid to the cream mixture before pouring the cream slowly into the soup, stirring constantly. Continue to stir the soup over low heat until it thickens slightly. Add salt and pepper. Chill.

Gazpacho

A friend asked for the definitive recipe for this famous cold soup. Such a thing probably doesn't exist, even in Spain, where there are hundreds of variations of what is practically a national dish. Here is one version, light and colorful and easy to adapt to whatever kitchen tools you have available.

10 medium tomatoes, very ripe
1 large green bell pepper
1 large yellow onion
1 large clove of garlic
2 cucumbers, or 1 large English
   cucumber
4 tablespoons olive oil
3 tablespoons red wine vinegar
1 tablespoon salt
pepper
8 ice cubes
3 slices of French bread

Peel tomatoes by immersing them in boiling water for ten seconds, then stripping off the skin. Halve them and squeeze out the seeds. Halve and seed green pepper. Peel cucumbers, halve them lengthwise and remove the seeds with a spoon. Peel garlic and onion.

Chop tomatoes, pepper, onion, cucumber and garlic, either by hand or in a food processor or blender. If you use a blender, which purees rather than chops, hand-chop two tomatoes and about two tablespoons each of the onion, pepper and cucumber to stir into the soup after it has been blended.

Stir in the olive oil, vinegar, salt and a generous amount of freshly-ground pepper. Add ice cubes and chill the soup in the refrigerator for several hours. Garnish each serving with a few cubes of bread, which have been cut into half-inch cubes and fried until golden in a little olive oil.

Senegalese Soup

What this soup has to do with the West African country of Senegal is hard to say, but the rich combination of cream, curry and chicken has become a hot-weather classic.

4 cups chicken broth
½ cup yellow onion, chopped
2 cups cooked chicken, finely chopped
2 teaspoons curry powder
1 large tart apple, such as Pippin or Granny Smith, peeled
1½ cups light cream
4 egg yolks
1 teaspoon salt
white pepper

In a heavy two-quart saucepan, simmer onion, cooked chicken, curry powder and chicken broth for ten minutes. Puree in a blender, food processor or food mill with the apple. Put back in the saucepan over low heat. Beat the eggs and cream together and pour them in a thin stream into the saucepan, stirring constantly. Cook and stir the soup over medium-low heat until it thickens slightly. Add salt and pepper. Chill for several hours before serving.

Avocado and Watercress Soup

This is a rich and creamy soup that involves no cooking. It is ideal before a simple meal of cold meat and salad.

1 large avocado
2 cups watercress, leaves and small stems, coarsely chopped
2 cups chicken stock
3 tablespoons scallions, chopped
⅓ cup lemon juice
1 cup plain yogurt
1 cup milk or half and half
1 teaspoon salt
white pepper
Tabasco

In a blender or food processor, puree avocado, watercress and scallions. Add chicken stock and yogurt, and blend until smooth. Transfer to a large bowl, add lemon juice and seasonings, and thin to taste with milk or half and half. Chill for several hours before serving.

Cold Beet Soup

This soup is ridiculously simple to make and comes out a startling magenta color.

2 cups sliced beets
1 quart buttermilk
½ cup chives, chopped
1 teaspoon salt
white pepper

You may use either canned or fresh beets. If you use the fresh, boil them until tender, then peel and slice them. In a food processor or blender, puree the beets with the buttermilk. Stir in chives, salt and white pepper. Chill.

Cheddar Cheese Crackers

Crisp, spicy crackers are a good accompaniment to any cold soup.

½ pound sharp, dry cheddar, grated
¼ pound butter, softened
1½ cups flour, sifted
¼ tsp. cayenne
½ tsp. dry mustard
½ tsp. salt

Preheat oven to 350 degrees. Work all the ingredients together with your hands. On a lightly-floured surface, shape the dough into a cylinder about 1½″ in diameter. Transfer to a piece of wax paper, and chill the dough in the refrigerator for at least half an hour. With a sharp knife, cut the dough into round slices ¼″ thick. Bake them on an ungreased cookie sheet for 10 to 12 minutes. Remove from the sheet with a spatula, and let them cool on a rack. Store in an airtight container.

9

SALAD DAYS

One of the nicest things about France, particularly southern France in the middle of the summer, is a few simple words that appear on almost every menu: Hors d'Oeuvres Variés. These are not hors d'oeuvres in our sense of a bite-sized morsel to be eaten when standing up at a cocktail party. Rather, they are cold dishes of many different kinds, salads made of meats and fish but mainly of the freshest local vegetables.

In a simple cafe, hors d'oeuvres variés are apt to be nothing more complicated than some grated carrots, beets in a vinaigrette dressing, grated celery root in a spicy mayonnaise and a hard-boiled egg dabbed with mayonnaise. A bit of tuna fish or a couple of sardines might be additional touches to this appetizer course.

At the other end of the gastronomic scale, there are restaurants where the hors d'oeuvres variés can number in the dozens and are really the most important part of the menu. In midsummer, sitting outside under the olive trees of Provence, the diner's task is simply to choose from the multitude of cold foods offered to him.

Classically, each different dish will be presented in a rectangular porcelain dish called a ravier. The raviers will be arranged on a buffet table or will be served from a rolling cart.

At the most elaborate restaurant of this type that I have ever seen, eighteen—we counted—first courses were served in sequence. Even though each serving was hardly more than a bite or two, a simple bit of grilled meat was more than enough as a main course, and none of us had any room for dessert.

Most of these cold dishes make ideal picnic foods. They can be cooked ahead and should be eaten at room temperature. They are full of flavor and freshness because most of them are made from summer produce.

Similar dishes are served in other Mediterranean countries. In Italy, when the streets are sweltering in midsummer, the cool, dim restaurants display their freshly-made cold dishes near the door, like bright, luminous jewels to tempt the passersby. In Turkey and other Middle Eastern countries, the array of cold dishes can number in the hundreds, alluring even the appetite made finicky by months of heat and humidity.

11

Obviously, an array like this is an achievement possible only in restaurants, where there are many hands to work on dozens of dishes. How many do you have to make? For a casual picnic, one cold vegetable dish, accompanying cold or grilled meat, may be enough. For an elaborate outdoor meal, anything from two or three of these salads to a dozen would be impressive.

If you do make a number of cold salads, you need nothing more than some sliced salami, bread and fruit to complete the meal. On the other hand, some of these salads—those that contain a large proportion of meat or fish—can be main dishes on their own. A Salade Niçoise is a fine summer supper that combines fish and vegetables in one bowl.

If you do decide to serve these salads as a main course, you may want to present them a little more elaborately, in a bed of lettuce on a wide, round platter, for instance.

However you display them, these cold dishes can be the most varied and distinctive parts of your menu.

Tomato Aspic

A homemade tomato aspic is a far cry from the canned aspics one usually has. Making it with pureed tomatoes, rather than tomato juice, gives it a more interesting texture and a fresher flavor. An aspic like this can be served by itself, as an accompaniment to cold meats and salads, or in a ring shape, filled with chicken or shrimp salad or a mass of watercress in a mustardy vinaigrette dressing.

4 cups tomato pulp (about 10
    very ripe tomatoes, peeled,
    seeded and coarsely chopped)
¼ cup lemon juice
2 teaspoons salt
pepper
¼ teaspoon sugar
⅛ teaspoon cayenne pepper
2 tablespoons fresh herbs, such as
    basil, tarragon or chives,
    chopped fine
2 tablespoons gelatin

Puree tomatoes in a blender, food processor or food mill. Dissolve gelatin in lemon juice, and add to tomatoes. Season with salt, pepper and herbs. Pour into a ring mold, and chill until set; this will take about 3 – 4 hours. Just before serving, invert mold over large flat plate. Cover with dish towel wrung out in hot water to warm mold until aspic drops out of mold.

Sweet and Sour Onions

2 pounds small white boiling
  onions
3 tablespoons olive oil
¼ cup dry sherry
¼ cup wine vinegar (sherry
  vinegar, if possible)
2 tomatoes, peeled, seeded and
  coarsely chopped
1 teaspoon thyme
1 bay leaf
1 clove garlic
½ cup raisins
1 teaspoon salt
pepper

Blanch onions for 5 minutes in
boiling water. Drain and peel
away outer skin. In a heavy casserole, combine onions and all
other ingredients. Cover and
cook slowly until onions are
barely tender. Uncover and cook
slowly until onions are tender and
liquid has turned into a thick
glaze. Cool.

Mushrooms in Tomato Cream

1 pound mushrooms
½ cup crème fraiche (see page
  51), or a combination of ¼ cup
  sour cream, ¼ cup heavy
  cream
1 tablespoon tomato paste
1 medium clove garlic, peeled
  and lightly crushed
¼ teaspoon salt
2 tablespoons parsley, chopped
pinch of Cayenne pepper
1 head Boston lettuce
2 tablespoons lemon juice

Combine crème fraiche or sour
cream and cream with lemon
juice, salt, garlic, tomato paste,
parsley and cayenne. Chill, then
remove garlic clove. Brush or
wipe mushrooms clean. Slice
them ¼" thick and immediately
stir them into sauce so that they
do not discolor. Chill, and serve
in a bowl lined with lettuce leaves.

Artichokes With Parsley and Mint

I have usually done this recipe
with the little tiny artichokes
about an inch long. If you can't
find them, use larger artichokes,
quartered.

3 pounds artichokes
1 cup chicken stock
½ cup olive oil
½ cup parsley, chopped
¼ cup mint, chopped
½ lemon
1 teaspoon salt
pepper

Trim artichokes, slicing off prickly
tops and stem ends and removing
outer leaves. If you are using
small artichokes, leave them
whole. If you are using larger artichokes, quarter them and remove the choke with a spoon;
drop them in water mixed with a
little vinegar as you work so that
they will not discolor. Heat olive
oil in a heavy casserole, put in artichokes and stir until they are
well-coated with oil. Add chicken
broth, lemon juice and the lemon,
parsley, mint, salt and several
grinds of black pepper. Cover the
pot partially and simmer gently
until artichokes are tender. This
usually takes about 30 minutes
but will vary according to the size
of your artichokes. The liquid will
have reduced to a thick sauce.
Allow the artichokes to cool and
serve at room temperature.

Rice Salad

Rice salad is a staple of French picnics. It is an ideal way to extend a couple of ripe tomatoes, some herbs and a can of tuna. The resulting dish looks pretty and will feed six people with ease.

Rice salads are obviously an open invitation to the improvisor who wants to use up bits and pieces of food that are already in the refrigerator. That's fine, but be wary of combining too many unrelated tastes in one bowl. The two recipes that follow produce salads that taste entirely different, with just a few harmonious ingredients for flavor.

Rice Salad with Tomatoes and Basil

1 cup raw rice
3 medium tomatoes, seeded, peeled and diced
1 green bell pepper, seeded and diced
3 tablespoons olive oil
1 tablespoon of vinegar,
2 tablespoons fresh basil, chopped
2 tablespoons parsley, chopped
1 teaspoon salt
pepper

Cook the rice in five quarts of boiling, salted water until it is just tender. Drain it and rinse briefly in cold water. While it is still lukewarm, stir in olive oil, vinegar, salt and pepper. Let the salad cool, then add tomatoes, green pepper, basil and parsley.

Rice Salad with Tuna and Anchovies

1 cup raw rice
½ cup mayonnaise
2 tablespoons lemon juice
1 tablespoon white wine vinegar
3 tablespoons scallions, chopped
1 7-ounce can of tuna
2 tablespoons parsley, chopped
3 anchovy fillets, chopped
1 tablespoon capers
1 teaspoon salt
pepper

Cook the rice in salted water until it is just tender. Drain it and rinse briefly in cold water. While it is still lukewarm, add mayonnaise, lemon juice, vinegar, salt and pepper. Let it cool for a few minutes, then gently stir in tuna, scallions, anchovy fillets, capers and parsley.

Chicken and Rice Salad

¼ pound fresh mushrooms
¼ cup lemon juice
½ cup olive oil
2 tablespoons fresh tarragon, or 1 teaspoon dried tarragon
1 cup raw rice
1½-2 cups cooked chicken, cut in strips
3 medium tomatoes, peeled, seeded and cut in strips
1 green bell pepper, halved, seeded and cut in strips
1 teaspoon salt
pepper
¼ cup parsley, finely chopped

Brush mushrooms clean and slice them ¼" thick. Combine olive oil, lemon juice, salt, tarragon and several grinds of black pepper, and marinate the mushrooms in this mixture for an hour or more. Cook the rice until just tender, drain and rinse briefly in cold water. While the rice is still lukewarm, stir in mushrooms and their marinade. Add the tomatoes, pepper and chicken. Just before serving, sprinkle the salad with parsley.

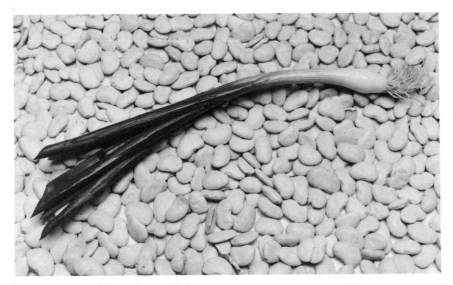

Rice-Stuffed Tomatoes

2 cups raw rice
12 medium tomatoes or 6 large ones
1 large yellow onion, chopped fine
3 tablespoons fresh mint
2 teaspoons oregano
¾ cup olive oil
2 teaspoons salt
pepper

Preheat oven to 350 degrees.

Slice tops off medium tomatoes or halve large ones. Squeeze out seeds and scoop out pulp with a spoon, leaving walls of tomatoes about ½″ thick. Chop the pulp to add to filling. Salt the tomatoes lightly with about 1 teaspoon of salt, and invert them to drain on paper towels while you prepare the filling.

Cook rice in five quarts of boiling salted water until barely tender. Drain and rinse briefly in cold water. While it is still warm, stir in ½ cup of olive oil. Add onions, mint, oregano, tomato pulp, 1 teaspoon salt and pepper. Fill the tomatoes with the rice. Put them in a shallow baking dish; they can be quite crowded, as they shrink while cooking. Pour water and olive oil carefully around them; liquid should come up to about one-third the height of the tomatoes. Bake for 35—40 minutes, until tomatoes are tender but have not split. Cool and serve them from the baking pan.

Ham, Turkey and Cheese Salad

¼ pound boiled ham
¼—½ pound cooked turkey or chicken
¼ pound Gruyere cheese
½ cup celery
¼ cup scallions
¼ cup parsley, chopped
½ cup creamy vinaigrette (see page 47)
1 head butter lettuce

Cut ham, turkey, cheese, celery and scallions into matchstick slices about 1½″ long. Gently stir in chopped parsley and vinaigrette. Serve on a bed of lettuce leaves in a salad bowl.

White Bean Salad

2 cups cooked or canned white beans
1 large clove of garlic, peeled and lightly crushed
¼ cup lemon juice
2 tablespoons scallions, chopped
2 medium tomatoes, peeled, seeded and cut in ½″ cubes
1 tablespoon fresh mint, chopped
1 teaspoon salt
pepper

If you cook the beans, soak them overnight, then cover with water and simmer them, covered, with a clove of garlic until they are tender. Drain them and let them cool. If you are using canned beans, drain them of the liquid in the can and rinse them in running water before preceeding with the recipe. Combine all other ingredients in a bowl, and stir in beans. Remove garlic clove before serving.

15

Ceviche

It was a big disappointment on a recent trip to Mexico to discover that many of the beach restaurants were serving something that they called ceviche but was an unappetizing blend of mushy fish, tomato sauce, peas and onions. I suspect that it came out of a can. This recipe is something else entirely, combining fresh fish, lime and lemon juice (in which the fish marinates, becoming opaque and firm without cooking) and a few distinctive spices. I like the contrast between the lean, spicy fish and the rich, buttery avocado on the side.

1½ pounds fresh, firm, white-fleshed fish
1 cup lime juice or a combination of lime and lemon juice
½ cup olive oil
1 cup red onion, thinly-sliced
1 cup tomatoes, peeled, seeded and cut in ½" cubes
2 hot jalapeño chilis, canned or fresh, chopped fine
2 tablespoons fresh coriander leaves, chopped
1 teaspoon salt
3 ripe, medium avocados

Cut fish into 1" cubes and marinate in the lime or lime and lemon juice for at least 2 hours in the refrigerator, stirring occasionally so that all surfaces of the fish become opaque white. Add olive oil, onion, tomatoes, chili peppers, fresh coriander and salt to fish and marinade, and let it all marinate a little while longer before serving. Serve either in half an avocado or with avocados sliced around it.

Tomato Salad with Feta Cheese

This is a decorative platter of fresh vegetables, inspired by traditional Greek salads.

6 large ripe tomatoes
1 large English cucumber (or 2 regular cucumbers)
1 large red onion
1 cup imported, brine-packed feta cheese
½ cup vinaigrette (see page 47)
½ cup olives, preferably Greek or Italian

Slice tomatoes and onion. Peel, seed and slice cucumber. On a round platter, arrange tomato slices in overlapping circles. Arrange cucumbers on top, then onion slices, then crumble feta cheese over all. Pour vinaigrette dressing over all, and surround with olives (which may be pitted or not, as you prefer). If you wish to take this on a picnic, arrange all the vegetables and cheese in layers in a covered bowl, top with olives and pour the vinaigrette over just before serving.

Tabbouleh

This is a Middle Eastern dish that is ideally suited to outdoor meals. It can be served decoratively in a shallow round dish lined with Romaine lettuce leaves and sprinkled with a ring of finely-chopped parsley, but it's equally delicious served right out of the kind of covered plastic container that fits in a picnic basket or a backpack.

1 cup cracked bulgur wheat
2 cups parsley, washed, dried and chopped fine
3 large tomatoes, cup into ½" dice
¼ cup scallions, chopped
¼ cup fresh mint, chopped
¾ cup olive oil
½ cup lemon juice
2 teaspoons salt
pepper

Soak bulgur wheat in 2 cups of warm water for 30 minutes or more. Drain, then squeeze dry in a kitchen towel. Put in a large bowl. Add parsley, tomatoes, scallions, mint, olive oil, lemon juice, salt and pepper. Stir thoroughly. Serve with Romaine lettuce leaves, Arab pocket bread or thinly-sliced French bread to scoop it up.

Salade Niçoise

This is a favorite summer dish in France, especially along the Mediterranean coast in July and August, when thousands of Parisians arrive to jostle each other for spaces on the beaches, jam the narrow highways that hug the cliffs above the sea and eat beautiful food like this. Traditionally, it's a first course, but I like it as a meal in itself.

1 pound string beans
2 pounds boiling potatoes
2 cups tomatoes, sliced, or halved cherry tomatoes
½ cup olives, preferably Greek or Italian
1 head butter lettuce
1 cup red onion, sliced thin
1 seven-ounce can of tuna
2 tablespoons shallots or green onions, chopped
1 cup olive oil
⅓ cup wine vinegar
2 tablespoons capers
6 anchovy fillets, chopped fine
1 teaspoon salt
pepper

To make vinaigrette, start by dissolving salt in the vinegar. Then pour in olive oil slowly, stirring constantly. Add capers and anchovy fillets and a generous amount of freshly-ground pepper.

Blanch string beans in salted boiling water until they are barely tender. Remove them from the water, drain and run cold water over them to stop them from cooking. In a bowl, stir them with a tablespoon of vinaigrette. Steam or boil potatoes until tender. While they are still warm, peel and cut them into thick slices. Pour about ¼ cup vinaigrette over them, add chopped shallots or scallions and stir or shake them gently to coat with dressing.

Slice tomatoes and red onions and pit olives. Assemble the salad by lining a wide, shallow bowl with washed and dried lettuce leaves. Spoon in potatoes in a mound in the center. Surround them with tomatoes and string beans. Crumble the tuna over the potatoes, and arrange onion slices and olives on top. Pour remaining dressing over all.

Chicken Salad

4 cups cooked chicken, cubed
½ cup mayonnaise
1 tablespoon curry powder
1 cup water chestnuts, sliced
½ cup raisins
1 cup grapes, halved
1 cup walnuts, coarsely chopped
1 teaspoon salt
pepper

Combine chicken, mayonnaise and curry powder, stirring well to coat the chicken. Soak raisins in hot water for ten minutes to soften them. Drain, and add to chicken, along with walnuts, grapes, water chestnuts, salt and pepper. This makes a good, unusual sandwich when it is used as a filling for pita bread.

Marinated Green Peppers

Peeling peppers is something of a bore, but the process definitely brings out a sweet taste in the vegetables. Two different methods are described below.

4 large bell peppers, either all
    green or a combination of red
    and green
¼ cup olive oil
1 large clove garlic, peeled and
    lightly-crushed
1 tablespoon red wine vinegar
1 teaspoon salt
pepper
2 medium tomatoes (optional)
½ cup feta cheese (optional)

Peel the peppers. One way, excellent when you do not have too many peppers, is to spear the stem end with a long-handled fork and hold the pepper over an open flame until it is dark brown and puffed on all sides. Let it cool, then pull off the skin. Another method, preferable when you have large numbers of peppers to peel, is to put them about 2″ under the broiler flame. Turn them so that all sides are browned and puffed. Cool and peel them. Remove the seeds and inner membranes, and slice the peppers into lengthwise slices ½″ wide. Put them in a bowl, stir in olive oil, vinegar, salt, garlic and a generous amount of freshly-ground black pepper, and let them marinate for several hours.

Although peppers are good by themselves, especially as an accompaniment to grilled meats, you may expand and elaborate this salad by adding 2 tomatoes, peeled, seeded and cut into long slices and ½ cup of feta cheese, crumbled and stirred gently into the peppers. Be sure that the feta is the imported, brine-packed variety.

Ratatouille

In restaurants all over France in July and August, this pungent stew of summer vegetables is a staple. It can be eaten hot, but it is more often eaten at room temperature. Ratatouille tastes better the day after it is made, when the different flavors have had a chance to blend together.

1 eggplant
4 large zucchini or 6 small ones
2 green bell peppers, seeded and
    sliced thin
6–8 medium tomatoes, seeded
    and coarsely chopped
2 large yellow onions, sliced thin
2 large cloves garlic, chopped
6 tablespoons olive oil
1 tablespoon salt
pepper

Wash but do not peel eggplant and zucchini; cut both into ½″ dice. Salt with 1 teaspoon of salt and let the vegetables drain in a colander for a half hour. Squeeze

dry with paper towels. Heat 2 tablespoons olive oil in a heavy frying pan until a haze forms above it. Add eggplant, and cook at high heat, stirring often, until it is lightly-browned and tender. Remove the eggplant to a heavy casserole.

Add two tablespoons olive oil to frying pan, add zucchini and cook until almost tender. Add to casserole, and sprinkle with 1 teaspoon salt and a few grinds of pepper.

Put 2 tablespoons olive oil in the frying pan, and add garlic, onions and peppers. Cook until they are almost soft. Stir in tomatoes; raise heat and cook for 5 minutes. Add 1 teaspoon salt and several grinds of pepper. Stir vegetables into casserole of zucchini and eggplant. Cook over medium heat, uncovered, for 20 minutes, stirring occasionally so that vegetables do not stick to the pot. There

should not be much liquid at the end of the cooking. Cool.

Lentil Salad

This is a typically French approach to leftovers, so good that it is worth starting from scratch to make it.

2 cups lentils
1 teaspoon salt
2 cloves garlic, peeled and lightly crushed
1 cup red onion, chopped
1 cup parsley, chopped
1 cup vinaigrette with mustard (see page 48)

Simmer lentils, salt and garlic in 5 cups water until they are just tender but not mushy; this should take about 25 minutes. Allow to cool. Remove garlic. Stir in onion, parsley and vinaigrette.

Beef Salad

Although many people consider boiled beef, served with a horseradish or tomato sauce, one of the world's great, simple delicacies, others look forward even more to what comes the next day—boiled beef salad.

To prepare beef:

1 three-pound piece of stewing beef, such as brisket or rump roast

2 carrots	10 peppercorns
1 onion	1 teaspoon thyme
2 turnips	2 teaspoons salt
4-5 sprigs parsley	
1 bay leaf	

Put all ingredients in a heavy casserole with a tight-fitting cover. Cover with cold water. Bring to a simmer, and cook, covered, for 2 hours, never allowing the liquid to come to a boil. Turn the meat once during cooking. If you are not going to serve it immediately, let beef cool in liquid.

To prepare salad:

1½ pounds boiled beef (about 4 cups)
1 cup red onions, quartered and thinly sliced
4 boiling potatoes
1½ cups tomatoes, seeded and diced, or cherry tomatoes, halved
2 cups parsley, chopped
1 cup mustardy vinaigrette (see page 48) or Sauce Ravigote
salt
pepper
1 head butter lettuce

Boil or steam potatoes until they are just tender, and peel and slice them. While they are still lukewarm, pour half the vinaigrette over them, and stir or shake gently.

Cut beef into half-inch chunks, free of all fat. Mix together beef, potatoes, onions, tomatoes, parsley and the rest of the dressing. Taste for seasoning and add additional salt and several grinds of black pepper. Serve in a bowl lined with butter lettuce.

Herbed Tomatoes

This recipe rewards you for searching out ripe, firm, mid-summer tomatoes and fresh herbs. While it is more interesting to have a combination of different herbs, you can also do it with just one easily available herb such as parsley, chives or basil.

6 medium tomatoes
4 tablespoons shallots or green
   onions, chopped fine
1 cup fresh herbs, such as tarragon, chives, chervil and
   parsley, chopped fine
1 cup vinaigrette (see page 47)
1 tablespoon salt
pepper

You may either halve the tomatoes or slice the tops off about ½" down; halving them is perhaps prettier, but keeping them whole makes them easier to transport to a picnic. In either case, gently squeeze the seeds out of the tomatoes. Sprinkle the cut side with salt and freshly-ground pepper, then with chopped shallots or green onions. Sprinkle

herbs on top, and then pour vinaigrette dressing in each one.

Potato Salad

This is a French-style potato salad, at its best when you can use plenty of fresh tarragon. If you can't have that, substitute fresh chives or parsley.

2 pounds boiling potatoes
½ cup chicken broth
½ cup olive oil
½-1 cup fresh herbs, coarsely
   chopped
1 teaspoon salt
pepper
¼ cup white wine vinegar

Boil potatoes until they are just tender; they will hold their shape better if they are not overcooked. As soon as possible, peel them and slice them about ⅓" thick. While they are still warm, toss them gently with the chicken broth and olive oil, then add vinegar, salt and pepper. Allow to cool, then stir in herbs.

Cold Pasta with Tomatoes and Basil

This utterly-simple recipe depends on the freshness of the ingredients. Don't try it unless you have ripe red tomatoes, fresh basil and flavorful olive oil.

1 pound pasta, preferably butterflies, spirals or medium
   shells
3-4 large ripe tomatoes, peeled
   and seeded
½ cup olive oil
½ cup fresh basil leaves, coarsely
   chopped
1 teaspoon salt
pepper

Cook the pasta in salted water until it is just tender. Drain and rinse briefly in cold water. Add olive oil while pasta is still lukewarm. Cut tomatoes into ½" dice. Let pasta cool to room temperature before stirring in tomatoes, basil, salt and a generous amount of freshly-ground pepper.

Cold Pasta Primavera

This recipe was inspired by a wonderful hot pasta dish that was created by a French restaurant in New York and immediately became very popular.

1 pound pasta, such as spirals, butterflies or medium shells
4 cups fresh vegetables, including two or more of the following —asparagus, green beans, peas and zucchini
6 medium tomatoes
¾ cup olive oil
1 large clove garlic
½ cup pine nuts
½ cup fresh basil, chopped
1 teaspoon salt
pepper

Peel asparagus and cut into one-inch lengths, halving them lengthwise if they are large. String beans and cut them into one-inch lengths. Quarter zucchini lengthwise and cut into one-inch sections. Shell peas. Cook all the vegetables until just crisp in boiling, salted water; this should take about three minutes.

Drain them and rinse in cold water to stop them from cooking.

Peel, seed and cut tomatoes into one-inch cubes. In a frying pan, heat 2 tablespoons olive oil with the garlic, finely chopped. Add the tomatoes, and cook gently for 3 minutes. Season with salt and a generous amount of freshly-ground pepper.

Toast pine nuts in 1 tablespoon olive oil over low heat. Cook the pasta in a large amount of salted water until it is barely tender. Drain and rinse in cold water. While it is still lukewarm, toss with ½ cup olive oil. In a large bowl, stir together pasta, tomatoes and vegetables. Finally, add basil and pine nuts.

Cold Noodles with a Chinese Flavor

Unlike the above versions of cold pasta, this has a distinctly Oriental flavor and takes advantage of some of the specialties available in Chinese delicatessens.

½ pound vermicelli (preferably Chinese noodles)
1 cup barbecued pork, cut in matchstick slivers (or you may substitute ham)
1 cup cooked chicken, cut in matchstick slivers
¼ cup scallions, cut in matchstick slivers
¼ cup fresh coriander leaves, chopped
1 tablespoon Chinese sesame oil
2 tablespoons Chinese hot chili oil
2 tablespoons soy sauce
¼ cup walnuts, shelled and halved
1 tablespoon salt

Cook the noodles in salted water until just tender. Drain and rinse under cold water. Toss with sesame oil, chili oil and soy sauce. Add pork, chicken, scallions, walnuts and coriander leaves.

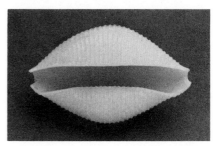

HARDBOILED AND OTHERWISE

There is nothing wrong with a plain hardboiled egg, particularly if it has been carefully prepared, simmered until the yolk is just cooked, then removed immediately from the hot water and cooled so that an ashy gray ring doesn't form around the yolk. With coarse salt and fresh pepper, a hardboiled egg deserves the traditional place it has had in picnic baskets.

But it is not the only kind of egg that belongs at an outdoor meal. Hardboiled eggs can become stuffed eggs with just a little work. They can be coated with green mayonnaise, the way the French serve them as a first course. Eggs are the main ingredient in every quiche and in that interesting Anglo-Saxon creation called the bacon and egg pie. The Spanish tortilla, an omelette filled with potatoes and onions, is yet another way to bring eggs to the picnic.

Yes, eggs do spoil in hot weather, but they're not so temperamental that you should avoid using them.

Kept cool, not cold, cooked eggs survive happily for several hours, and that's sufficient for most picnic plans.

The Useful, Ubiquitous Quiche

A quiche is simply a pie crust filled with beaten eggs, cream and almost any flavoring your imagination devises, from the traditional eggs and bacon known as Quiche Lorraine to cheese, smoked salmon, onions or leftover ratatouille.

Once you have your pie crust fitted into a 9-inch pan (such as the French pans with straight, fluted sides and a removable bottom, a porcelain quiche dish or—ideal for picnics—an inexpensive, disposable aluminum pie pan), the first step is to prebake it. Line the shell with wax paper or foil, fill it with beans, rice or aluminum pie weights to keep the pastry from rising, and bake it for 15 minutes in a 375 degree oven. Then remove the weights, paint the inside of the shell with beaten egg white and return it to the oven for 5 more minutes. These steps will prevent a soggy crust.

It takes about 3 cups of filling for each 9-inch quiche. Start with 3 large or extra-large eggs. Add your flavoring, such as mushrooms, spinach or cheese. Then bring the filling up to the three-cup mark by adding cream or half and half; you may need a little more or less than the following recipes specify.

The quiche is done when it is firm in the center and very lightly browned on top, usually after 25 to 30 minutes in a 375 degree oven. It will puff up when hot, then subside as it cools. Quiches can be eaten hot, cool or in between. They are better if they have not been refrigerated, but in very hot weather they should be kept in an ice chest.

Cheese and Tomato Quiche

1 nine-inch pie shell, prebaked
1 tablespoon olive oil
6 medium tomatoes, peeled, seeded and chopped
1 large yellow onion, chopped
1 large clove garlic, chopped
1 teaspoon thyme
1 teaspoon salt
pepper
½ cup Gruyère cheese, grated
3 large eggs
1 cup cream, approximately

Preheat oven to 375 degrees.

In a frying pan, heat olive oil, add onions and garlic and cook over moderate heat for about 5 minutes, being careful that garlic does not burn. Add tomatoes, salt, pepper and thyme. Cook over moderate heat until you have a quite dry and highly-flavored puree. Let cool. Meanwhile, beat eggs until they are light. Add grated cheese and tomato puree. Finally, add cream, enough so that the total amount of filling is about 3 cups. Pour carefully into pastry shell and bake for about 30 minutes, until filling is firm and top is puffed and lightly browned.

Mushroom Quiche

1 nine-inch pie shell, prebaked
1 pound mushrooms
4 tablespoons sherry or Madeira
3 tablespoons shallots or green onions, chopped
2 tablespoons butter
1 teaspoon salt
3 large eggs
½ cup cream or half cream, half milk, approximately
pepper

Preheat oven to 375 degrees.

Slice mushrooms ¼-inch thick. Melt butter in a large frying pan. Add chopped shallots, stir and let cook for a minute. Add mushrooms, sherry or Madeira, salt and pepper. Stir, and cook over medium heat for about ten minutes, until mushrooms are tender and liquid has completely evaporated. Let cool. Beat three eggs and add mushrooms. Add enough cream or half and half so that filling measures three cups. Pour into pie shell and bake for 25 to 30 minutes, until the center is firm and the top is puffed and very lightly browned.

Onion Quiche

1 nine-inch pie shell, prebaked
5 cups onions, sliced (about 5 medium yellow onions)
3 large eggs
½ cup Swiss cheese, grated
3 tablespoons butter
½-1 cup cream or half cream, half milk, approximately
¼ tsp. nutmeg
2 teaspoons salt
pepper

Preheat oven to 375 degrees.

Slice onions ¼-inch thick. Melt butter in a large frying pan. Add onions and cook over medium heat, stirring occasionally, until they are soft and deep gold in color.

Beat eggs, and add onions, grated cheese, nutmeg, salt and a generous amount of pepper. Stir in enough cream or cream and milk so that the filling measures 3 cups. Pour the filling into the pie shell, and bake for 25 to 30 minutes, until the center is firm and the top is puffed and lightly browned.

Spinach Quiche

1 nine-inch pie shell, prebaked
1½ lb. fresh spinach (about 3 bunches) or 2 packages frozen spinach
3 tablespoons shallots or green onions, chopped
2 tablespoons butter
3 large eggs
½ – 1 cup cream or half cream, half milk, approximately
1 teaspoon salt
⅛ teaspoon nutmeg
pepper

Preheat oven to 375 degrees.

If you are using fresh spinach, rinse it carefully in several changes of cold water and remove thick stems. Without drying leaves, place them in a large saucepan, cover and cook over medium heat, stirring occasionally, until spinach is just tender.

Drain spinach in a colander, pressing to remove as much water as possible. Chop coarsely. If you are using frozen spinach, cook according to package directions and drain.

Melt butter in a frying pan. Add shallots and cook for a minute, before adding spinach, salt, nutmeg and a few grinds of pepper. Cook over medium high heat, stirring frequently, until all liquid has evaporated. Beat eggs and add spinach. Add enough cream or cream and milk so that the mixture measures 3 cups. Pour into pie shell and bake for 25 to 30 minutes, until the center is firm and the top is puffed and very lightly browned.

Spanish Tortilla

This is not a tortilla in the sense of a Mexican corn cake but a tortilla in the Spanish sense of an omelette. This one is robust enough to serve as a main course, and it can be eaten hot, cold or in between. Don't be dismayed by the large amount of oil involved; most of it gets poured off and can be reused.

4 medium boiling potatoes, about 2 cups, peeled and sliced ¼" thick
1 onion, about 1 cup, coarsely chopped
1 cup ham, diced (optional)
1 cup olive oil, or a combination of olive oil and peanut oil

4 eggs
1 tsp. salt
pepper

In an 8" non-stick frying pan, heat the oil until a haze forms over it. Add the potatoes and cook them over medium heat, covered, for about 5 minutes. Gently stir in the onions and ham, and cook for about 10 to 15 minutes longer, adjusting the heat so that the onions don't burn, until the potatoes are tender. The pan will be full, but the potatoes and onions will cook down.

Pour off as much of the oil as possible, using the lid to hold in the potatoes and onions.

Beat the eggs with the salt and a generous amount of pepper. Pour the eggs into the pan with the potatoes and onions. Cover and cook over very low heat, shaking the pan occasionally so that the eggs don't stick. When the bottom side of the omelette is lightly browned, slide the pan under the broiler for a few moments to cook the top. After a minute or two, when the eggs are completely cooked, invert the omelette onto a serving plate.

Hard-boiled Eggs Al Pesto

6 hardboiled eggs
6 tablespoons pesto sauce
2 tablespoons mayonnaise

You can either make your own pesto sauce by the following recipe or use the frozen pesto available in Italian delicatessens and some supermarkets.

Halve eggs lengthwise and remove yolks. In a small bowl, mash the yolks with the pesto sauce and the mayonnaise. Taste for seasoning; depending on your sauce, you may or may not need additional salt and pepper. Refill egg whites with yolk mixture.

Pesto

2 cups basil leaves
1 teaspoon salt
2 teaspoons chopped garlic
2 tablespoons pine nuts
½ cup olive oil

In a blender or food processor, puree basil, salt, garlic and pine nuts. With the machine still running, add olive oil in a thin stream. You may also do this with a mortar and pestle, first crushing solid ingredients into a paste, then adding oil. If you wish to use this sauce for hot pasta, add ½ cup Parmesan cheese at the last minute. This addition is unnecessary if you are using the pesto for the stuffed eggs in the recipe above. Pesto freezes well.

SANDWICHES FOR GROWNUPS

Sandwiches are not just for children. Let the kiddies glue themselves together with peanut butter and jelly if they like, but don't forget that adults like sandwiches, too.

Pan Bagna

This is a salad in a sandwich. As in a lot of traditional Provençal foods from the south of France, there are apparently infinite numbers of variations on the theme, depending on the time you have or your fondness for garlic or what happens to be sitting around in the kitchen. Even purists need not fear that lightning will strike if they improvise on this recipe.

1 loaf French bread
4 large tomatoes, sliced ½" thick
1 large red onion, sliced ¼" thick
1 large clove garlic
1 tin anchovies
1 green pepper, seeded and
    sliced thin
2 tablespoons capers
½ cup olives, preferably Greek or
    Italian, halved and pitted
½ cup olive oil
1 teaspoon salt
pepper
string

Peel and lightly crush garlic, and let it marinate in the olive oil; garlic-lovers should do this several hours ahead of preparing the sandwich to get a strong garlic taste.

Cut the loaf of French bread in half lengthwise and hollow it out, leaving the walls about ½" thick. Generously brush the cut surfaces with the garlic-flavored olive oil. On one half of the loaf, spread the tomatoes, and salt and pepper them quite generously. On top of them, layer the onion and green pepper slices, the anchovies, capers and olives. Put the other half of the loaf of bread on top and tie the whole thing together with kitchen string as tightly as possible. The longer this sits, with the juices and flavors melding together and permeating the bread, the tastier it will be. Cut it in thick 3" slices to serve.

Do-It-Yourself Sandwiches from the Supermarket

For the really last-minute picnic, the answer is to forget about cooking and simply do some rapid shopping. Do-it-yourself sandwiches are fun for everyone. Provide everyone with a plate, knife and napkin, and let them create their own masterpieces.

Give them a choice of—

Bread, such as French rolls, rye bread, French bread or hamburger buns
Ham
Salami
Turkey
Cheese, such as Gruyere or Monterey Jack
Tomatoes, sliced
Red onions, sliced
Green peppers, sliced
Watercress
Avocado, sliced
Fresh bean sprouts
Pitted olives
Salt
Pepper
Mayonnaise
Butter
Mustard, preferably Dijon-style
Chutney

A Tortilla Feast

This is a do-it-yourself feast with a Mexican flavor. It can be done anywhere that you can heat the tortillas briefly, whether for a few seconds on each side over a barbecue, over an open flame on a camp stove or steamed for a minute over boiling water. Keep them warm by wrapping them in a kitchen towel and putting them in a covered dish or basket.

Put out the warmed tortillas with dishes of slivered cooked chicken, pork or turkey, Monterey Jack cheese cut in matchstick slivers, shredded lettuce, chopped tomatoes, chopped onions, sour cream and the following two sauces. Then let people roll their own. Provide plenty of napkins; this is messy, delicious food.

These two sauces are similar to those served in huge carved bowls at a taco stand in Zihuatanejo on the Pacific coast of Mexico. The sauces looked so good that we ignored the cautions about eating food from outdoor stands in Mexico. It was delicious, and we lived to tell the tale, with no ill effects.

Salsa Cruda

4 medium tomatoes, peeled and chopped
3 tablespoons white onion, chopped
2 tablespoons fresh coriander leaves, chopped
2 hot jalapeño peppers, either canned or fresh (about 2 teaspoons, chopped)
1 teaspoon salt
pepper

Combine all the ingredients and taste for seasoning. Remember that hot peppers seem to get hotter as the hours pass.

Avocado Sauce

2 ripe, medium avocados
3 tablespoons fresh coriander leaves, chopped
3 tablespoons onions, chopped
3 tablespoons canned mild green chilis, chopped
1 hot jalapeño chili, canned or fresh, chopped (about 1 teaspoon)
1 teaspoon salt

Peel and remove the pits of the avocados. Chop coarsely and combine with all other ingredients. Cover with plastic wrap to keep the avocados from turning black.

Meat Loaf in a Loaf

1 pound ground chuck
½ pound ground pork
½ pound ground turkey or veal
3 tablespoons chives, chopped
½ cup onions, chopped
½ cup bread crumbs
2 eggs
1 tablespoon salt
pepper
2 tablespoons Worcestershire
   sauce
1 loaf French bread
4 tablespoons butter, softened

3 tablespoons Dijon-style mustard

Preheat oven to 375 degrees.

Halve the loaf of French bread, and hollow it out, leaving the walls about ½" thick. Mix ½ cup of the bread crumbs you have removed with the ground meats, chives, onions, eggs, salt, pepper and Worcestershire sauce. If you wish to taste for seasoning, fry a tablespoon of the meat mixture in a little butter; this is to avoid eating raw pork.

Form the meat into a loaf about the same size and shape as the loaf of bread. Bake for one hour in a small roasting pan. While it is cooking, spread the cut surfaces of the French bread with butter and mustard. As soon as the meat loaf is cooked, place it inside the loaf of bread, and tie the two halves of the loaf together as tightly as possible with kitchen string. Weight the loaf down for at least ½ hour to force the juices into the bread. Cut in thick slices to serve.

THE MAIN ATTRACTION

Main courses for outdoor meals come from different cuisines and countries all over the world. We have the English to thank for the meat pies that are a staple in their pubs. The Middle East is responsible for flaky pastries, while Argentina gets the credit for the rolled steak called matambre. Italy's summer meals often star veal tonnato, while the French serve patés. From the United States come simple, impressive recipes for fish baked in foil and cold roasts of pork and lamb.

Leg of Lamb with Sorrel

This is a cold version of a delicious dish developed by San Francisco food writer Jane Benet one day when she was confronted with a surfeit of sorrel.

1 six-pound leg of lamb, boned and butterflied
6 cloves garlic
2 cups sorrel, stemmed and chopped coarsely
1 cup mushrooms, chopped fine
2 teaspoons salt
pepper
1 tablespoon cooking oil
Preheat oven to 375 degrees.

Simmer the unpeeled cloves of garlic for about ten minutes in water to cover. They will become soft enough to squeeze out of their skins like a paste. Remove the stems from the sorrel and chop the leaves coarsely. Chop mushrooms very fine. Heat 1 tablespoon oil in a small frying pan and cook the mushrooms over high heat for 2–3 minutes. Lay the piece of meat open and spread garlic paste on it. Salt and pepper it. Spread sorrel and mushrooms on top. Tie meat into as neat and compact a roll as possible, using plenty of string to prevent the filling from leaking out. Rub the outside of the rolled roast with salt and pepper. Roast it for 1 to 1½ hours, depending on how well-cooked you like your lamb. Remove from the oven, and cool at room temperature.

Bacon and Egg Pie

This is classic Anglo-Saxon picnic food. If you don't make your own puff paste, you can sometimes buy it from French bakeries or you can roll out the dough from Pepperidge Farm's frozen patty shells. This recipe will feed at least eight or ten people as part of a picnic menu.

1 pound puff paste
10 eggs
½ pound Canadian bacon or
  ham, sliced thin
½ cup chives, chopped
½ cup parsley, chopped
1 teaspoon salt
pepper

Preheat oven to 450 degrees.

Divide puff paste in half. On a floured surface, roll out one half so that it is large enough to line the bottom and sides of a 9″×9″ brownie pan or similar sized baking pan with sides at least one inch high. Lay the pastry in the pan, and put half the Canadian bacon or ham on it. Break nine eggs on top.

With a fork, stir them gently so that the yolks are broken but yolks and whites are still separate, not beaten into a homogeneous mass. Sprinkle with chives, salt and pepper. Cover with the rest of the bacon or ham.

Roll out the rest of the puff paste and lay it loosely on top, attaching top and bottom crusts by pressing them together with the tines of a fork. You may decorate the top by making leaves and other motifs out of any scraps of rolled-out pastry. Paint the top of the pie with an egg beaten lightly with a little water.

Place the pie on the lower shelf of a 450 degree oven, and turn the heat down to 400 degrees. The pie will be ready when the top is golden brown, in about 30 minutes. To take on a picnic, do not refrigerate; wrap in layers of newspaper or dish towels to keep pie warm.

Matambre

This is beef, marinated, rolled around eggs and vegetables and braised in liquid. It is an Argentinian specialty, originally developed as a meat dish that would keep well during long journeys across the vast plains. Although it is traditionally eaten as an appetizer in the Argentine, it makes a handsome main course for a picnic.

Although the Argentinians usually make matambre with skirt steak, it is difficult to get large enough pieces of skirt steak in this country. You will probably have to use flank steak.

3 pounds flank or skirt steak,
  butterflied
½ cup vinegar
½ cup wine
¼ cup oil
2 bay leaves
4 cloves garlic, chopped
6 cooked carrots
4 eggs, hard-boiled
2 cups spinach or chard leaves,
  washed and stemmed
1 large onion, sliced
½ cup parsley, chopped
1 cup cooked peas (optional)
2 – 3 dried red peppers, crumbled, or 2 teaspoons red pepper flakes
2 teaspoons salt
2 cans beef bouillon

Have your butcher butterfly the flank steak, or split it in half horizontally with a long, sharp knife, leaving the meat joined at the edge of one long side. Marinate the meat for several hours in vinegar, wine, oil, bay leaves and garlic.

Open the flank steak out flat. If you are using two, place them end to end, overlapping them by a few inches. On the meat, sprinkle the red peppers, marinade and salt. Then distribute the spinach or chard, eggs, carrots, onion, peas and parsley evenly on the meat.

Roll the meat into a tight roll, being careful that the stuffing does not leak out, and tie it in several places. Place it in a heavy pot, preferably an oval casserole, and pour in bouillon and water to reach at least halfway up the meat. Simmer, covered, over low heat for one hour, turning the roll once.

Allow to cool in the liquid. To take on a picnic, wrap the matambre in foil. Cut in half-inch slices at the time of serving.

Pork Roast with Apples and Prunes

This recipe for pork roast with a fruit filling is equally good hot or cold.

1 pork loin, about three pounds boned and tied
1 cup pitted prunes
½ cup sherry
1 large tart apple, such as Granny Smith or pippin
1 tablespoon salt
pepper
2 tablespoons cooking oil

Preheat oven to 325 degrees.

Soak prunes in sherry for 30 minutes. With a long, narrow knife (such as a ham-slicing knife), a sharp skewer or a sharpening steel, make a tunnel lengthwise down the center of the pork roast. Peel and core apple, and cut it into eighths. With the handle of a long wooden spoon, push the fruit down the tunnel in the meat, alternating prunes and apples. Rub the roast with salt and pepper. Heat the oil in a heavy roasting pan on top of the stove, and brown the meat, turning it several times so that it is evenly colored. Roast it in the oven for 1½ hours. Let cool, preferably without refrigeration. To take it on a picnic, wrap it in foil and slice it in ½" slices just before serving. Serve with currant jelly or chutney.

Pork Roast with Garlic and Rosemary

2 – 3 pound pork loin roast, boned
1 large clove garlic
1 tablespoon rosemary
¼ cup olive oil
2 teaspoons salt
pepper

Preheat oven to 425 degrees.

Cut garlic into thin slivers, and insert them in pork loin, using the point of a knife to make slits in the meat. Using your hands, rub the meat with oil, salt, pepper and rosemary. Brown the roast in a heavy roasting pan, turning so that all sides are evenly-browned. This will take about 15 minutes. Turn oven down to 325 degrees, and roast the meat for about 1½ hours. Cool outside refrigerator. If meat must be refrigerated, wrap it in a double layer of foil before putting it in refrigerator.

Lamb Pie

In this delicious main course pie, ground lamb is given a Middle Eastern flavor with the addition of raisins, cinnamon and pine nuts and is encased in buttery, crisp sheets of filo dough. Filo pastry, also known as strudel dough, is available in many supermarkets and in Middle Eastern delicatessens. Despite its almost transparent, fragile appearance, it is easy and fun to use.

3 cups cooked lamb, ground or
    chopped
1 large yellow onion, chopped
1 large clove garlic, chopped
3 tablespoons olive oil
3 tablespoons pine nuts
1 teaspoon allspice
1 teaspoon cinnamon
¼ cup raisins
¼ pound filo dough (about 10
    sheets)

½ cup butter, melted
1 teaspoon salt
pepper

Preheat oven to 375 degrees
In a large frying pan, heat the olive oil until a haze forms above it but it is not smoking. Add the pine nuts and, over moderate heat, let them cook until they turn golden brown. With a slotted spoon, remove them from the oil and drain them on a paper towel.

Add onion and garlic to the oil and cook until the onion is soft. Add lamb, spices, salt, raisins and a generous amount of freshly-ground pepper. Cook for about ten minutes over low heat. Add pine nuts, and taste for seasoning.

Keep filo dough covered with a clean, damp kitchen towel to prevent it from drying out. Line a buttered 9″×12″ baking dish with three layers of filo, brushing each layer with melted butter. Spread half the lamb filling over the filo. Add three more layers of filo, brushing each one with butter. Spread the other half of the lamb, and finish off with three or four more layers of filo, brushing each with butter and making the top one as neat as possible.

Bake for 45 minutes, or until pastry is golden brown.

You may also make individual pastries from this recipe. To do so, cut filo sheets into lengthwise strips about five inches wide. Lay one (or two, if they are difficult to separate) on a horizontal surface. Brush with melted butter. Place 3 tablespoons of lamb about 2½″ from the left-hand edge. Lift up bottom left-hand corner and fold filo diagonally over filling, so that the corner meets a point on the top edge about five inches in from the end. Fold again along the straight edge, then diagonally, as if you were folding a flag, to form a triangular pastry. Continue until you reach the end of the strip of filo. Bake pastries on a cookie sheet until golden brown.

Although these lamb-filled pastries can be eaten cold, they are better if they can be reheated for a few minutes before serving. If no oven is available, cook the lamb pie just before you leave for the picnic, and wrap it well in foil and several layers of newspaper.

Chicken Vinaigrette

This is more than a salad and makes a decorative main course, with the herbed chicken on a bed of watercress, surrounded by new potatoes and cherry tomatoes. If you want to take it on a picnic, carry all the elements separately —the chicken marinating in the vinaigrette—and assemble the platter just before serving.

Chicken:

1 three-pound chicken
1 onion, quartered
2 carrots, cut in two-inch lengths
2 celery branches, cut in two-inch
  lengths
2 – 3 branches parsley
2 teaspoons thyme

Vinaigrette:

½ cup olive oil
¼ cup wine vinegar
½ cup tarragon, chopped
2 tablespoons mint, chopped
3 tablespoons chives, chopped
3 tablespoons parsley, chopped
½ teaspoon salt
pepper

Garnish:

12 cherry tomatoes, halved
12 small red new potatoes
2 tablespoons olive oil
1 large bunch watercress

Place chicken in a large pot, and cover with cold water. Add carrots, celery, onion, parsley and thyme. Bring to just below a boil, cover and simmer until chicken is tender (about an hour), without letting water come to a boil. Remove chicken from water, drain and let cool until it is lukewarm. With your fingers, remove meat from the bones, trying for neat, skinless pieces about two inches long.

Boil or steam potatoes until tender. While they are still warm, stir them with 2 tablespoons olive oil. Mix vinaigrette. Whisk vinegar and salt together, and continue to whisk while adding oil slowly. Stir in chopped herbs. Pour over chicken.

Remove thick stems from watercress and arrange on a platter. Before serving, put chicken on watercress and surround with potatoes and tomatoes.

Marinated London Broil

1 two-pound piece of London broil, at least 1″ thick
¼ cup olive oil
¼ cup lemon juice
¼ cup red wine
2 tablespoons soy sauce
1 teaspoon thyme
2 cloves garlic, chopped
½ teaspoon pepper

Combine olive oil, lemon juice, red wine, soy sauce, thyme, garlic and pepper. Marinate meat in this mixture for several hours at room temperature or overnight in the refrigerator, turning occasionally. Broil 2″ from the flame for about 10 minutes per side, for rare meat, or according to your taste.

This is delicious hot and even better cold, sliced very thin and served with a choice of Dijon-style mustard or the herb sauce on page 49.

If you wish to barbecue a similar piece of meat, substitute a 2-pound boneless chuck roast and marinate it in the same way. Brush the roast with the marinade while it is cooking.

Marian's Fruited Beef

This unusual recipe for boiled beef with dried fruits comes from Czechoslovakia. If you take it on a picnic, put beef and sauce in a covered container, then slice it just before serving.

1 three-pound piece of bottom round of beef, trimmed of all fat
2 yellow onions, chopped
1 stalk celery, chopped
6 medium tomatoes
2 tablespoons peanut oil
¾ cup dried apricots
¾ cup raisins
2 carrots, sliced thin
¼ teaspoon allspice
½ teaspoon dry mustard
1 cup red wine
1 clove garlic
1 bay leaf
4 – 5 sprigs of parsley
1 tablespoon salt
pepper

Preheat oven to 350 degrees.

Rub meat with salt, pepper and the cut side of a halved clove of garlic. Brown meat in oil in a heavy casserole or Dutch oven, and remove it from the pot. Adding more oil if necessary, cook chopped onion and celery over moderate heat until they are soft. Add tomatoes and wine, and simmer for 5 minutes. Return the meat to the pot, and add raisins, apricots, carrots, bay leaf, parsley, allspice and mustard. Liquid and other ingredients should come at least half way up the side of the meat; if not, add either water or wine. Cover pot tightly and cook in the oven for 2 hours, keeping liquid at just a simmer, until meat is very tender.

Allow to cool, preferably without refrigerating. Slice about ⅓″ thick, and serve each slice with a spoonful of sauce, which will be thick.

Rabbit Paté

This rabbit paté is a specialty of my mother-in-law, who has been making it for special occasions for many years. It is like no other paté I have ever tasted; it is almost completely fat free, surrounded by a delicious jelly made from the rabbit bones. Note that this is not the kind of paté you spread on crackers or bread but is intended to be sliced about ½" thick and served like any cold meat. A French potato salad is a good accompaniment.

1 2½ – 3 pound rabbit (including the liver)
½ pound boneless pork, preferably loin
½ pound boneless veal, preferably scallops or steaks that can be cut in thin horizontal slices

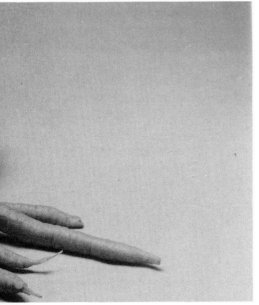

1 pound ground pork
2 carrots
1 leek
4 – 5 sprigs parsley
½ cup shallots, chopped fine
1½ teaspoons thyme
3 bay leaves
1 tablespoon salt
pepper
½ cup Cognac
leaf fat, enough to line a 6"×8" oval terrine (this is fine white fat, available in sheets from your butcher)

Bone the rabbit, cutting the meat into neat slices (as big as possible) about ⅓" thick. Trim the veal and pork of all fat and slice about ⅓" thick.

Put the rabbit bones in a saucepan with carrots, peeled and sliced, and the white of leek, sliced, ½ teaspoon of the thyme, 1 bay leaf, 1 teaspoon salt, several grinds of pepper, parsley, and 1 quart of water. Simmer, partly covered, for 1½ to 2 hours. Chill and remove congealed fat from the top.

While it is cooking, mix the ground pork with shallots, ½ teaspoon thyme, the rabbit liver, finely-chopped, 1 teaspoon salt, pepper and 2 tablespoons Cognac.

Preheat oven to 375 degrees. Line the terrine with leaf fat, and

put a bay leaf at the bottom. Layer the meats in the following order, sprinkling lightly with salt and pepper where indicated: sliced pork, salt, pepper and 2 tablespoons jelly, ⅓ of the ground pork, ½ of the rabbit slices, salt, pepper, 2 tablespoons jelly and 2 tablespoons Cognac, ⅓ of the ground pork, veal, salt and pepper and 2 tablespoons jelly, ground pork, remaining rabbit slices, salt, pepper and 2 tablespoons each of jelly and Cognac. If you have any left over, continue to layer in the same fashion. With your fists, press down on the meats so that they are packed into the terrine as tightly as tightly as possible. On top, put another sprinkling of salt, ½ teaspoon thyme, and 1 bay leaf, and cover it with leaf fat. Pour remaining jelly and Cognac on top.

Cover the terrine closely and place it in a larger oven-proof pan, such as a roasting pan, in which you can pour a couple of inches of water. Bake in a 375 degree oven for 2½ hours, checking occasionally to make sure water has not evaporated; if it has, replace it to the same level. Remove from oven, remove cover and weight down the paté (some heavy cans of soup on a double layer of foil make a good weight) while it cools. With a spoon, remove excess fat on top.

Veal and Ham Pie

This is an easy version of a classic English pub dish.

Pie crust for 9″ double-crust pie
½ pound veal
½ pound ham
2 eggs, hardboiled
1 egg white
4 tablespoons fresh herbs, such as parsley, tarragon and chives, chopped fine, or a combination of 3 tablespoons chopped parsley and 1 tablespoon dried fines herbes
1 tablespoon olive oil
¼ cup chicken stock
2 tablespoons Cognac
¼ teaspoon grated lemon rind

Preheat oven to 375 degrees.

Divide the pie crust in half. Roll out half the crust and lay it in a 9″ pie or quiche pan. Fill with rice, beans or aluminum pie weights on a piece of wax paper, and bake for 15 minutes in the oven until the crust is lightly-browned.

Take it out of the oven, remove weights and paper, and paint the crust with egg white beaten with a teaspoon of water. Return to oven for 5 minutes. Remove from oven and cool while you proceed with the rest of the recipe.

Cut veal into small cubes, removing all fat. Grind ham or chop it

very fine. Mix ham, veal, herbs, olive oil, chicken stock, Cognac, lemon rind and several grinds of pepper in a bowl, combining the ingredients thoroughly.

Slice eggs horizontally in ½″ slices. Place half of meat mixture in the pie crust, and distribute egg slices on top. Cover with the other half of the meat mixture. Roll out the other half of the pie crust and lay it on top of the pie, cutting it so that it overlaps the bottom crust about ½″ all around. Crimp edges together to form a decorative rim.

Bake for one hour at 375 degrees on the middle rack of the oven. Cool before serving.

Turkey Tonnato

This is a variation on a popular Italian dish that appears often at summer buffets. It is traditionally made with a loin of fine white veal, which is often difficult and invariably very expensive to obtain in most parts of the United States. This recipe takes advantage of the inexpensive turkey roasts that are now available in many supermarkets. Although the directions on packaged turkey roasts usually suggest roasting, I think you get a more flavorful and moist-textured result by poaching the turkey with vegetables.

1 three-pound boneless turkey roast
1 large carrot, peeled and cut into 1" sections
1 large onion, peeled and quartered
4 – 5 sprigs fresh parsley
1 teaspoon thyme
1 tablespoon salt
10 peppercorns
1 seven-ounce can of tuna
1 cup olive oil
⅓ cup lemon juice
6 anchovy fillets
2 tablespoons capers

Place turkey roast in a heavy casserole. Surround with carrot, onion, parsley, thyme, salt and peppercorns. Cover with cold water. Simmer, covered, for about one hour. Let cool in liquid.

Meanwhile, make the sauce, preferably in a blender or food processor. Puree tuna and anchovy fillets, then add olive oil in a thin stream while machine is running, as if you were making a mayonnaise. Stir in lemon juice and capers. Thin the sauce with a little of the turkey-cooking liquid, so that the sauce is almost as thin as heavy cream.

Slice the turkey in ¼" slices, and arrange on a platter. Coat with the sauce, cover with plastic wrap and refrigerate, preferably overnight. Just before serving, garnish with a few more capers, lemon wedges and sprigs of parsley.

Foil-Baked Fish

This method of cooking salmon or any large fish eliminates the need for a fish poacher and results in a moist, flavorful fish. The measurements given here are for a six-pound fish, but the recipe can be adjusted for any size fish.

1 six-pound fish, such as salmon, cleaned and scaled
2 tablespoons peanut oil
2 lemons, sliced thin
2 onions, sliced thin
1 bunch parsley
½ cup Vermouth or white wine
2 teaspoons salt
pepper
Lemon and parsley for garnish

Preheat oven to 450 degrees
Lay fish on a double layer of heavy-duty foil about three times the size of the fish. Measure fish at its thickest point to estimate cooking time; it will take approximately 10 minutes in the oven per inch of thickness. Rub outside of fish with peanut oil. Sprinkle inside cavity with salt and pepper. Fill cavity with lemons, onions and parsley. Moisten the fish with Vermouth or wine, and wrap the fish in the foil, crimping it closed so that no liquid can leak out. Place on middle rack of oven, and cook for required time.

Remove from oven and unwrap foil. Remove skin from both sides of fish, turning carefully with your hands or two wooden spatulas, and place on serving platter. Cool and serve, garnished with more lemons and parsley, with Green Mayonnaise (see page 48.) or Cucumber Sauce (see page 51).

THE OPEN FLAME

I like to think that barbecuing began when some unnamed caveman dropped a hunk of raw meat on an open fire, forgot about it for a while and then discovered that it tasted pretty good that way.

Of course, since then things have gotten a lot more complicated. From the electric-powered rotisserie to the gas-powered barbecue, gadget-mad Americans have invented hundreds of gadgets to make barbecuing into an activity almost as technical as cooking indoors.

Besides a stunning array of equipment, many barbecue fanatics are armed with an array of theories. Each one believes that he alone—barbecue fanatics tend to be men—has the secret barbecue sauce that will enhance everything. He alone holds the one true method of lighting the coals and knows the exact moment when the coals are exuding the right amount of heat.

All of this is fine and fun, but barbecuing need not be so complicated if you don't want it to be. A small barbecue, as simple as the inexpensive Japanese hibachi, can be the basic tool for a good meal anywhere from a city terrace to the wide open spaces.

A heavy oven mitt, a long-handled fork, a long-handled brush and some flat-bladed skewers (if the skewers are round, the food will keep sliding around on them, making it impossible to cook things on all sides) are other necessary items.

This simple equipment will not produce food that tastes as if you had cooked it on your stove, but that's hardly the point of outdoor cooking.

The real goal in barbecuing is to make sure that your food still tastes like what it is, not like a dry, charred morsel slathered with the ubiquitous barbecue sauce that makes everything taste alike.

41

One way to do this is to marinate the meat beforehand. The marinade can be mixed ahead in your kitchen, and meat and marinade transported together in a strong plastic bag or a container with a tight-fitting cover. Many marinades contain lemon juice, wine or yogurt, all of which tenderize, preserve and flavor at the same time.

Marinades also help you to use less expensive cuts of meat. The monster porterhouse, charred and rare, is a magnificent meal that most people can afford rarely, if at all. Fortunately, there are less costly meats that are just as good, especially if they contain quite a lot of fat to counteract the drying effect of open-air cooking. For instance, the best barbecued hamburgers always seem to be made from the cheapest—i.e., fattiest—ground meat. Chuck roast, at a fraction of the price of sirloin, becomes a delicious steak on the grill.

Another trick is to cook over moderate heat. A solid coating of carbon is not an asset. Rumor has it that it's also unhealthy for you—one more reason to keep the flames down.

Spiedini

The first time I suggested grilling skewers of bread and cheese over the barbecue, everyone looked dubious. We did it anyway, and the results were eaten up in about three minutes. Try it, and don't even consider skipping the anchovies, which give the bland combination of bread and cheese the piquancy it needs. Spiedini are a good way to quell the hunger pangs of the masses while the steak is cooking.

1 loaf French bread
1 pound Mozzarella cheese
1 cup olive oil
1 tin anchovy fillets

Cut bread into one-inch cubes. Cut cheese into ¾-inch cubes. Cut anchovy fillets into thirds, and pour any remaining oil from the can into the olive oil. Dip each cube of bread into olive oil. On 6-8 skewers, line up ingredients in the following order: bread, anchovy, cheese, ending with an extra cube of bread. Grill the skewers over moderate coals until bread is crisp and cheese is melted. Scrape each skewer onto a plate.

Chicken Alla Diavolo

3 pounds chicken parts, preferably drumsticks and thighs
½ cup olive oil
½ cup lemon juice
2 teaspoons red pepper flakes
1 teaspoon salt
pepper

Combine all ingredients except chicken parts. Add chicken and marinate for several hours; you may put them in a large bowl or transport them to a picnic in a plastic bag. Barbecue over moderate coals for about 15 minutes per side.

Yogurt-Marinated Chicken

Yogurt, so the story goes, was developed by desert nomads as a dairy product that doesn't spoil in hot weather. That makes it an ideal ingredient for any picnic recipe. In the following marinade for barbecued chicken, the yogurt keeps the meat from spoiling, tenderizes it and gives it a delicious flavor that combines both sweet and spice.

2 three-pound chickens, cut into pieces
2 cups plain yogurt
1 teaspoon cumin
1 teaspoon cayenne pepper
2 cloves garlic, chopped
2 teaspoons salt
1 teaspoon allspice

2 teaspoons fresh ginger,
    chopped
pepper

Combine all ingredients except
the chicken; marinade should be
very highly-flavored. Marinate
chicken in yogurt mixture for several hours; if you are going to a
distant picnic spot, it is convenient
to put chicken and marinade in a
plastic bag that can be tied closed.
Barbecue chicken over moderate
coals for about 15 minutes on
each side, basting with marinade.
You may also do it ahead of time
under the broiler if you wish to
serve the chicken cold.

Barbecued Scallops and Mushrooms

2 pounds scallops
1 pound mushrooms
1 cup bread crumbs, preferably
    freshly-made
1 teaspoon salt
pepper
4 tablespoons butter
3 lemons

Brush mushrooms clean, and
halve them lengthwise. Melt 1
tablespoon butter in a frying pan,
and add the mushrooms. Over
moderately high heat, cook them
for 2 minutes, stirring frequently.
Place mushrooms and scallops on
6 flat-blade skewers. Mix together
bread crumbs, salt and pepper.

Just before cooking, brush scallops and mushrooms with 3 tablespoons melted butter, and dip the
skewers into the bread crumbs,
which you have spread on a plate
or a piece of wax paper. Barbecue over medium coals, for a
total of about 10 minutes, until
scallops are cooked through.
Serve with half a lemon per
skewer.

Barbecued Fish Skewers

2 pounds firm, white-fleshed fish, such as halibut
2 tablespoons olive oil
¼ cup lemon juice
¼ cup dry vermouth
1 tablespoon soy sauce
pepper
¼ pound bacon

Cut the fish into one-inch cubes. Marinate it for 2 hours in the olive oil, lemon juice, vermouth, soy sauce and a few grinds of pepper. Skewer them carefully, against the grain of the fish, alternating fish cubes with one-inch long slices of bacon. Barbecue over moderate coals for about 5 – 6 minutes, until fish is cooked and flakes away easily.

Barbecued Lamb

The following marinade for a butterflied leg of lamb results in a delicious piece of meat that can either be eaten just as it comes off the barbecue, hot or cold, or can be used for the souvlakia recipe that follows.

1 piece of lamb, preferably from the leg, about 3 pounds after being butterflied and boned
½ cup olive oil
⅓ cup lemon juice
1 large clove garlic, chopped
2 teaspoons oregano
2 tablespoons mint, chopped
1 teaspoon salt
pepper

Mix together all the marinade ingredients, and let the lamb marinate for at least 6 hours. Barbecue over medium coals.

Lamb Brochettes

3 pounds lamb, preferably from leg or shoulder, trimmed of fat and cut into 1" cubes
½ cup olive oil
⅓ cup lemon juice
1 large clove garlic, peeled and chopped
1 teaspoon rosemary
1 teaspoon thyme
1 teaspoon salt
pepper
½ pound bacon

Combine olive oil, lemon juice, garlic, rosemary, thyme, salt and several grinds of pepper. Marinate the lamb in this mixture, stirring occasionally, either overnight in the refrigerator or for several hours at room temperature. Arrange the meat on skewers, alternating a cube of lamb with ⅓ of a slice of bacon folded in two. Cook over moderate coals for about 10 minutes on each side, or until meat is done to your taste. Brush with left-over marinade
These are delicious with barbecued eggplant slices, which can be cooked at the same time and brushed with marinade or olive oil.

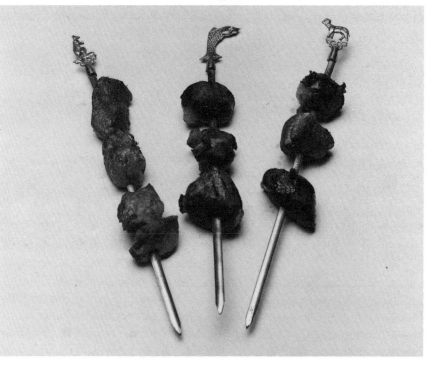

YEAR OF THE RAM 1919 . 1931 . 1943 . 1955 . 1967.

TAYLOR & NG © 1978 WIN NG

Souvlakia

Souvlakia is the hamburger of Greece. I first tasted it many years ago on an outdoor stand on the island of Mykonos. Since then, souvlakia stands, usually reeking of garlic and oregano, have opened up in cities all over America. The following recipe uses the marinated and barbecued lamb above. Thin slices of meat are put in the pockets of pita bread, now available in many supermarkets and at Middle Eastern delicatessens. Sliced tomatoes and onions and a yogurt sauce are then added. The result is a messy, delicious sandwich.

6 pocket breads, cut in half across the diameter
2 cups tomatoes, sliced thin
2 cups onions, sliced thin
2 cups yogurt
1 large clove of garlic, peeled and lightly-crushed
3 tablespoons fresh mint, chopped
1 teaspoon salt
pepper
To make yogurt sauce, combine yogurt, crushed clove of garlic, mint, salt and a few grinds of pepper in a small bowl, preferably 2 hours before serving. Remove the garlic before serving.

For a do-it-yourself souvlakia feast, put out the pita bread, heated slightly on the edge of the barbecue, the sliced onions, sliced tomatoes and yogurt sauce. Let each person build his own sandwich, assembling lamb, tomatoes, onions and final dollop of yogurt sauce in the pocket of the halved pita bread.

45

A SELECTION OF SAUCES

Just a few cold sauces are the key to transforming random leftovers into splendid salads, an ordinary hardboiled egg into a classic French hors d'oeuvre, a plain poached fish into an impressive centerpiece.

Most of those that follow are variations on three basic sauces—vinaigrette, mayonnaise and crème fraiche. Once you have these in hand, you can start adding other flavoring ingredients. You can also start combining them with each other; a mayonnaise can be thinned with a little vinaigrette, or a vinaigrette made thicker and smoother with crème fraiche.

Vinaigrette

⅓ cup wine vinegar
½ teaspoon salt
⅔ cup olive or peanut oil
pepper

In a small bowl or measuring cup, whisk together vinegar and salt until salt dissolves. Continue to whisk while you add oil in a thin stream. Add a generous amount of freshly-ground pepper.

Vinaigrette aux Herbes

1 cup basic vinaigrette
4 tablespoons fresh herbs, such as tarragon, chives, chervil and parsley, chopped fine

Sauce Ravigote

1 cup basic vinaigrette
4 tablespoons fresh herbs, chopped fine
1 tablespoon capers, chopped
1 tablespoon shallots, chopped
1 tablespoon cornichons, chopped

Combine all ingredients. This sauce, and the one that follows, are classical accompaniments to cold meat salads.

(Cornichons are small, pickled gherkins from France, available in gourmet departments.)

Mayonnaise

Undoubtedly there are still many Americans who think that all mayonnaise comes in jars. Many others know that you can make mayonnaise at home but believe that it is complicated and tricky. Certainly many cookbooks succeed in making it sound so.

Actually, making mayonnaise is a cinch, easily mastered by any reasonably-coordinated six-year old. The following recipe can be executed with a fork, a whisk or a blender. Personally, I prefer an electric hand mixer. Contrary to the prevailing advice about eggs at a certain temperature and special mixing bowls, I use eggs right out of the refrigerator and the nearest mixing bowl around.

The reason for going to even this amount of trouble is simply that homemade tastes better. Once you've got the habit, the white stuff in jars with its odd chemical taste will be strictly for emergencies and tuna sandwiches for the kids.

2 egg yolks
½ teaspoon prepared Dijon-style mustard
½ teaspoon salt
2 tablespoons wine vinegar or lemon juice
1 cup oil (I prefer peanut oil)
pepper

With a hand mixer, beat egg yolks, mustard and salt for one

minute in a mixing bowl. Beating constantly, add oil very slowly, at first drop by drop and then in a thin stream. Do not stop beating until the sauce has begun to solidify. When all the oil is incorporated into the sauce, add two tablespoons wine vinegar or lemon juice and a few grinds of pepper. Taste for seasoning.

If, perhaps because of very hot weather, the sauce refuses to "take" or solidify, start over again with two egg yolks, mustard and salt. Beat for one minute, then add your first, failed sauce, drop by drop. When this takes, begin to add oil slowly.

This basic recipe makes 1¼ cups of mayonnaise. If you need more, you may add up to a cup more of oil, increasing vinegar and seasonings at the end accordingly.

Once the basic mayonnaise is made, you can start adding to it. Some variations on the theme follow.

Mustard Mayonnaise

1 cup basic mayonnaise
2 tablespoons Dijon-style mustard
lemon juice
pepper

Stir into mayonnaise two tablespoons of mustard, some grinds of pepper and a few drops of lemon juice. This spicy sauce goes well with cold meats. It is also a good accompaniment to cold asparagus and broccoli, peeled and cooked briefly so that they are still crisp.

Green Mayonnaise

1 cup basic mayonnaise
4 tablespoons fresh herbs, such as chives, parsley, tarragon and chervil, chopped very fine

Stir herbs into mayonnaise, at least 1 hour before you plan to serve it.

This sauce is a classic with cold salmon. Stir in half a cup of plain yogurt to lighten it, if you wish. It is also a perfect dip for raw vegetables. Thinned with cream, it is an ideal sauce for mixtures of cubed, cooked vegetables.

Sauce Remoulade

This is no more than a green mayonnaise with some additions that turn it into a rich, spicy sauce that goes well with cold fish.

1 cup basic mayonnaise
4 tablespoons fresh herbs, such as parsley, chives, chervil and tarragon, chopped very fine
2 tablespoons capers, chopped
2 tablespoons cornichons, chopped
4 anchovy fillets, chopped

Stir all ingredients into mayonnaise.

Fresh Herb Sauce

This bright green sauce is a good accompaniment to cold meat, such as the marinated London Broil on page 36. Serve it, too, with barbecued fish or meat.

1 cup, firmly-packed, of two or more fresh herbs, such as chives, tarragon, chervil and parsley
3 anchovy fillets
2 egg yolks, hard-boiled
2 teaspoons capers
1 large clove garlic
¾ cup olive oil
1 teaspoon salt
pepper
In a mortar, blender or food processor, crush herbs, anchovies, capers, garlic and egg yolks into a smooth paste. Add olive oil, at first drop by drop and then in a fine stream, as if you were making a mayonnaise. Season to taste with salt and pepper.

Sauce Gribiche

1 cup basic vinaigrette
4 tablespoons fresh herbs, chopped fine
1 tablespoon capers, chopped
1 tablespoon shallots, chopped
1 tablespoon cornichons, chopped
1 hardboiled egg, chopped
2-3 anchovy fillets, chopped (optional)

Combine all ingredients. In France, this elaborate version of a vinaigrette is often served with hot or lukewarm cooked tongue, as well as with cold meats and salads.

Mint Sauce

This is not the vinegar and mint sauce the English love so with leg of lamb but a mint and yogurt sauce with a Middle Eastern flavor that goes well with grilled meat, especially lamb, either hot or cold.

1 cup plain yogurt
½ cup fresh mint, chopped
⅛ teaspoon cayenne pepper
⅛ teaspoon paprika
½ teaspoon salt
2 – 3 drops Tabasco
Combine all ingredients, preferably at least an hour before serving.

Hot Pepper Jelly

Hot pepper jelly, a traditional favorite in the Southwest, has recently become extremely popular all over the country. It belongs in a picnic basket because of its affinity with cold meats and poultry, including smoked chicken and turkey. Serve it, too, with cream cheese and crackers. The following recipe makes about three quarts, enough for many picnics.

2 cups green or red bell peppers, chopped fine
6½ cups sugar
1⅓ cups white vinegar
12 dried red peppers, crumbled, or 1½ tablespoons red pepper flakes
2 twelve-ounce bottles liquid pectin such as Certo

Seed and remove white fibers from peppers before chopping fine by hand or in a food processor. Put in a large, deep pot, along with the crumbled red peppers or pepper flakes, sugar and vinegar. Over medium heat, bring to a boil. Turn down the heat and simmer for ten minutes.

Strain contents of pot through several layers of cheesecloth that you've used to line a colander set over a second large pot. If you are using green peppers, you may at this point want to add a drop or two of green food coloring. Add pectin, and bring the mixture to a boil for one minute.

Remove to a convenient working area, where you have clean, warmed jars ready. Ladle jelly into the jars quickly, screw the tops on and turn the jars upside down on a surface covered with a folded dish towel. After a few minutes, turn upright.

Crème Fraiche

Crème fraiche—the thickened, slightly soured cream the French use for many of their cream sauces—is handy for picnics because it keeps well. It tastes good on fresh fruit, particularly berries, and it is also a useful basis for cold sauces and salad dressings. For instance, crème fraiche, mixed with a little white vinegar and dill, is delicious with sliced cucumbers.

1 teaspoon buttermilk
1 cup heavy cream

Mix buttermilk and cream together, and heat gently until it is just lukewarm. Pour into a container and leave, partially covered, at room temperature. Depending on the temperature in the room, it will take between six and twenty-four hours to thicken and acquire its distinctive soured taste. Refrigerated, it will keep for more than a week.

Cucumber Sauce

This subtle, pale green sauce goes well with barbecued fish or cold salmon.

1 cup crème fraiche or sour cream
1 large cucumber
2 tablespoons white wine vinegar
2 tablespoons fresh tarragon, chopped, or 2 tablespoons dried tarragon
1 teaspoon salt
white pepper

Peel, seed and chop cucumber very fine. Salt with ½ teaspoon salt and let drain in a colander for 30 minutes. Squeeze cucumber dry in a clean kitchen towel. Combine all ingredients, tasting for seasoning.

Creamy Salad Dressing

This is something between a mayonnaise and a vinaigrette—a smooth, spicy dressing that would be delicious with sliced raw mushrooms, cubed cooked chicken or boiled artichokes.

1 egg yolk
1 teaspoon mustard

1 tablespoon shallots, chopped very fine
½ cup peanut or olive oil
2 tablespoons wine vinegar or lemon juice
¼ cup cream or crème fraiche
½ teaspoon salt
pepper

Beat egg yolk, mustard and salt together in a mixing bowl or measuring cup with a small whisk. Still beating, add oil slowly, as if you were making a mayonnaise. Stir in vinegar or lemon juice, shallots, cream and pepper to taste.

SPLENDOR ON THE GRASS

All picnics are special, but some are more extraordinary than others. We have definite expectations, for instance, of a Fourth of July picnic, which must be resolutely American—no French fanciness here, no exoticism from Third World cuisines—and purely traditional.

Then there is the cold weather picnic. This could be a way to take advantage of a crisp, clear autumn day, like the Thanksgiving weekend lunch I once attended after a fox hunt in South Carolina. More likely, it's a skier's meal at the top of the mountain on a fine March day.

Finally, we offer the luxury picnic, an array of costly foods cooked and served with refinement. This would be the ideal accompaniment to a concert in the vineyards, Shakespeare in the park or chamber music in the country. It would also be a romantic menu for two, perhaps packed into a bicycle basket.

Picnic Deluxe

Here is a menu that seems to demand porcelain plates, stemmed glasses, linen napkins and a bottle of fine Cabernet Sauvignon. The recipes are designed to feed two people, since it's unlikely that one would serve this kind of food to large numbers of people.

Potted Shrimp
Casserole-Roasted Quail
Endive and Watercress Salad
Macaroons

Potted Shrimp

¼ pound butter
⅓ pound small bay shrimp, cooked and peeled
¼ teaspoon mace
¼ teaspoon nutmeg
¼ teaspoon salt
¼ teaspoon cayenne pepper

Clarify butter by melting it slowly in a small saucepan. Let it cool for a couple of minutes, until milky solids go to the bottom of the pan. Pour clear butter, leaving solids in the saucepan, into a small frying pan. Stir in mace, nutmeg, salt and cayenne pepper, mixing well to blend spices. Add shrimp and stir gently over moderate heat for one minute. Put this mixture into a small, covered container and chill for 24 hours.

Potted shrimp, an English specialty, are traditionally served with hot toast. At a picnic, far from a toaster, they are delicious on thin rounds of French bread or melba toast.

Casserole-Roasted Quail

Quail can become dry, uninteresting little morsels if you don't take some care in cooking them. The following method produces succulent little birds that can be eaten hot or cool.

4 quail, about 4 ounces each
4 slices of bacon
1 teaspoon garlic, chopped
1 cup white wine or Vermouth
1 tablespoon tomato paste
1 teaspoon salt
pepper
½ teaspoon paprika

Cut bacon slices into squares and cook them slowly in a heavy casserole until they render about two tablespoons of fat. Rub the quail with salt, pepper and paprika, and brown them over moderate heat in the bacon fat, turning them gently. When they are lightly browned, remove them from the pan. Add garlic, vermouth and tomato paste to the pan, stirring to blend ingredients. Return the quail to the pan, laying them on their sides, cover the pan and cook over low to moderate heat for 15 minutes. Turn the quail on their other sides, cover, and cook for 15 more minutes.

Remove quail from the casserole, and place them on pieces of aluminum foil large enough to wrap them securely. Remove bacon slices from the casserole and dis-card. Reduce the remaining liquid over high heat until there are about four tablespoons of liquid left. Pour one tablespoon of this sauce on each quail, and wrap each bird securely in foil.

Endive and Watercress Salad

2 large Belgian endive
1 bunch watercress
½ cup creamy salad dressing (see page 57), omitting shallots

Separate leaves of the endive, and cut them horizontally into squares. Remove watercress leaves from stems and discard stems. Combine watercress and endive with dressing, thinning with a little additional cream if necessary.

Macaroons

½ pound almond paste
1 cup powdered confectioner's sugar
2 egg whites
¼ teaspoon salt
1 teaspoon vanilla

Preheat oven to 350 degrees. Cut sheets of heavy unglazed paper, such as paper bags from the supermarket to fit two cookie sheets. With your fingers or a food processor, crumble almond paste and combine with sugar. Add two whites, one at a time, blending thoroughly. You should have a thick paste that is smooth but will hold its shape in a spoon; you may need to add a bit more egg white but be careful that it does not become too liquid. Put the mixture into a pastry tube and squeeze it out, one tablespoon at a time, onto pastry sheets covered with paper. Leave at least two inches between cookies as they will spread out while cooking.

Bake for 25 minutes. To remove cookies from paper, wet the back of the paper with a wet towel or run water over the back of the paper. Then gently peel the paper away from the cookies, and cool them on racks.

An All-American Fourth of July

There are no surprises here, just familiar favorites that most Americans love.

Sliced Tomatoes and Onions
Potato Salad
Cole Slaw
Crisp Fried Chicken
Chocolate Chip Cookies

Serve with a big bowl of cherries, a couple of sparklers per person and American beer and wine.

Cole Slaw

4 cups cabbage (red, green or a
combination of both), shredded
or coarsely chopped
½ cup mayonnaise
½ cup sour cream or plain yogurt
2 tablespoons vinegar
1 tablespoon prepared horseradish
1 teaspoon salt
pepper
1 teaspoon dill

Shred or chop cabbage. Combine
with all other ingredients, and
keep cool until served.

Potato Salad

4 cups boiled potatoes
½ cup mayonnaise
½ cup plain yogurt
1 teaspoon salt
pepper
2 tablespoons vinegar
2 tablespoons onion, chopped
2 tablespoons chives, chopped
2 tablespoons parsley, chopped

Boil potatoes until just tender,
cool, peel and cut into half-inch
cubes. Combine mayonnaise,
yogurt, salt, pepper and vinegar.
Add potatoes, onion and herbs to
this mixture, folding everything
together gently. Keep salad cool
until it is served.

Fried Chicken

This recipe produces chicken
that's very crisp on the outside,
moist and flavorful inside, and it's
not much more trouble than buy-
ing it from Colonel Sanders.

1 3-pound chicken, cut up
2 eggs
1 cup milk
2 teaspoons salt
1 teaspoon pepper
½ teaspoon paprika
2 cups flour
cooking oil

Beat together eggs and milk in a
bowl. Add 1 teaspoon salt and ½
teaspoon pepper. Mix together
flour, 1 teaspoon salt, ½ teaspoon
pepper and ½ teaspoon paprika,
and spread this on a plate.

In a frying pan large enough to
hold all the chicken pieces in one
layer, heat up enough cooking oil
to come up one half inch on the
chicken as it is cooking. Heat until
a light haze appears above it.

Dip each piece of chicken in the
egg and milk mixture and then in
the seasoned flour, turning to
make sure they are well coated.
As each piece is coated, place it in
the hot oil. Cook over high heat
until chicken is golden brown on
one side, then turn and brown it
on the other side. Then turn the
heat down to moderate, cover the
pan and cook for 20 minutes. Uncover the pan, raise heat and
cook for five more minutes. Cool
the chicken on paper towels before packing it for the picnic.

Chocolate Chip Cookies

¾ cup butter, softened
⅔ cup white sugar
⅔ cup brown sugar
1 teaspoon vanilla
2 eggs
1½ cups flour
½ teaspoon baking soda
¼ teaspoon nutmeg
½ teaspoon cinnamon
1 cup chocolate chips
1 cup walnuts, coarsely chopped

Preheat oven to 375 degrees.

Cream together butter and white
and brown sugar. Beat in two
eggs, combining thoroughly. Sift
together flour, baking soda, cinnamon and nutmeg before adding dry ingredients, a little at a
time, to eggs-butter-sugar mixture. Add vanilla, chocolate chips
and walnuts. For large cookies,
drop batter, one tablespoon at a
time, about two inches apart on
greased cookie sheets. Bake 10 to
12 minutes. Remove cookies from
sheets with a spatula and cool
them on racks.

A Skier's Picnic

The following menu is consciously high-calorie, to give a burst of strength to skiers who plan to spend the whole day on the slopes. The soup will stay hot in a Thermos bottle, and the frittata, prepared in the morning, is delicious at any temperature.

Black Bean Soup
Cheese-Stuffed Celery
Frittata

Additions to this menu might be sandwiches of thick slices of baked ham on French bread with butter and Dijon mustard and a selection of chocolate bars for dessert.

Cheese-Stuffed Celery

¼ pound Roquefort
¼ pound butter, softened
1 large bunch of celery

Mash together Roquefort and butter into a smooth paste. Wash celery and separate into stalks. Cut each stalk into three-inch lengths, and fill the cavity with Roquefort mixture. These can either be wrapped individually in foil or arranged in layers in a small covered box, with wax paper between each layer.

Black Bean Soup

1 pound black beans
1 onion, chopped
3 stalks of celery, coarsely chopped
2 tomatoes, unpeeled and chopped
1 ham hock, cut into two-inch sections
1 bay leaf
1 teaspoon salt
pepper
2 cans beef consomme or bouillon, or 3 cups beef stock

7 cups water
½ cup sherry

Combine all ingredients except salt and pepper in a large pot. Bring to a simmer, and cook over low heat for three hours, until beans are tender. Remove ham hocks, and put the soup through a food mill or a sieve, pressing with a large spoon to crush beans. Taste for seasoning, add salt, pepper and sherry. An optional garnish at the time of serving is a tablespoon of sour cream per portion.

Frittata

A Frittata, the Italian version of an omelette, is a splendid addition to a picnic, as well as a fine way to use different ingredients already in your kitchen. This version features Swiss chard and an optional addition of ham, but you might also enjoy experimenting with zucchini, browned onions, spinach or a thick saute of tomatoes and onions.

This recipe makes a large, important-looking frittata, to turn out on a round platter. Backpackers can cut it into individual wedges to wrap in foil.

For a smaller frittata, cut ingredients in half and cook in a six-inch pan.

4 cups Swiss chard leaves, cut in thin strips
3 tablespoons olive oil
4 ounces boiled ham, cut in thin strips (optional)
10 eggs
2 teaspoons salt
pepper

½ cup grated Swiss or Parmesan cheese
3 tablespoons butter

In a frying pan, heat olive oil, add chard leaves and cook, stirring frequently, until chard is wilted but still slightly crisp. If you are using ham, add it at this point and stir for a minute to combine thoroughly.

In a large bowl, beat eggs lightly. Stir in salt, a generous amount of freshly-ground pepper and grated cheese. Finally, add chard, mixing thoroughly so that the ingredients are evenly distributed. Melt butter in a heavy, ten-inch frying pan, preferably one with a non-stick surface. As soon as butter is melted, pour in the egg mixture.

Over very low heat, cook until the mixture is firm but still moist, about 20 to 25 minutes. To finish cooking the top, which may still be slightly liquid, put the pan under a hot broiler until the top is cooked. Loosen the frittata around the edges with a spatula and slide out onto a platter.

SOMETHING TO DRINK

Liquid refreshments at a picnic need be no more complicated than plenty of cold beer, soft drinks and jug wine, but there are a few alternatives.

Lemonade

There's no real reason for using lemonade mixes when making the real thing is so simple.

12 lemons
½ cup sugar
ice

In a gallon jug, put lemon juice and sugar. Stir until sugar is dissolved. Add lemon rinds, and fill the jug with ice. Shake well, and let the ice melt for a half hour or so before serving.

Iced Coffee

This recipe gives you a strong coffee syrup which you can mix with ice and water or milk at the time of serving.

¼ pound finely-ground coffee
3 tablespoons sugar

Mix coffee with 2 cups water in a saucepan. Stir well and heat to the boil. Remove from heat and leave for 15 minutes. Strain through a cloth into a saucepan. Add sugar and heat to the boil, stirring to dissolve sugar. Remove from heat and cool.

At the time of serving, pour two tablespoons of syrup over ice, and add milk or water to fill the glass.

Sangria

2 bottles red wine, such as
    California burgundy
1 large apple, cut in thin slices
2 peaches, cut in slices
1 orange, unpeeled, sliced thin
1 lemon, unpeeled, sliced thin
½ cup sugar
1 bottle champagne or soda water

Make a sugar syrup with sugar and enough water to cover. Heat and stir until sugar dissolves. Cool. Combine syrup with other ingredients, including any juice from the fruit. Chill. Serve sangria over ice, topped with about ½" of champagne or soda water, which is added to each glass as it's served.

Iced Tea

6 tea bags (Earl Grey is good)
4 tablespoons sugar
8 sprigs fresh mint
⅓ cup orange juice

Bring 2 quarts water to a rolling boil. Pour over tea bags, sugar and mint. After 5 minutes, remove tea bags, and let the tea cool. When it is cool, strain it into a pitcher and stir in the orange juice.

THE END OF THE AFFAIR

The all-American, winner-of-the-county-fair, star-of-the-bake-sale cake, layer upon layer, ebullient with sculpted waves of frosting, has no place at my picnic. Nor do chocolate eclairs, melting in the sun, or lemon meringue pies or any other elaborate confection.

Give me something simpler at the end of my outdoor feast. A bowl of fruit, either the way it came from the tree or marinating in its own juices, will be fine. So will a cookie or a cake, unadorned with thick frosting, that I can eat neatly, perhaps while wandering through the landscape.

Pecan Pie

This recipe is here for my husband, a Frenchman who generally has the usual prejudice in favor of all things French. He makes an exception for this all-American pie, willingly eating even the gluey versions sold at dime store lunch counters. This version is heavy on the pecans and has an added, optional, boozy touch of bourbon.

1 nine-inch pie shell, baked
   empty until lightly brown
4 eggs
1½ cups dark corn syrup
2 tablespoons melted butter
1 teaspoon vanilla
2 tablespoons bourbon
1½ cups pecans

Preheat oven to 375 degrees. To prepare pie shell, line it with wax paper and fill it with rice, beans or metal pie weights. Bake it in a 375 degree oven for about 15 minutes, until crust is lightly browned. Remove weights and allow crust to cool a few minutes before filling.

Beat the eggs lightly. Continue to beat while adding corn syrup. Stir in melted butter, vanilla, bourbon and pecans. Make sure that the pie shell has no leaks or cracks before pouring filling into it. Bake for about 40 minutes until filling is firm. Pecan pie keeps well, and the bourbon flavor seems to intensify.

Honey Cake

This is a Czechoslovakian recipe that was given to me by a friend who got it from her grandmother who lived in Prague. The family used to make it in large quantities and put it down in the cellar to age. The flavor does improve after a few days, and the cake keeps moist if you keep it wrapped in foil in a cool place or the refrigerator. Although this recipe specifies a square baking pan, it was traditionally made in loaf pans.

1⅓ cups rye flour, sifted
⅔ cup whole wheat flour, sifted
½ cup sugar
1 tablespoon bitter cocoa
1 teaspoon baking soda
½ teaspoon cinnamon
½ teaspoon ground cloves
½ teaspoon mace
½ teaspoon ground ginger
½ teaspoon ground nutmeg
½ teaspoon ground allspice
1 egg
⅜ quart milk
1 tablespoon butter
½ cup honey
½ cup ground almonds
1 tablespoon grated orange or
  orange and lemon rind

Preheat oven to 350 degrees.

In a big mixing bowl, combine all the dry ingredients. Lightly beat egg. Melt butter with honey. Making a well in the middle of the dry ingredients, gradually add egg, milk, melted butter and honey. Beat together well for several minutes with a big wooden spoon. Stir in almonds and orange rind. Pour into a greased 9″×9″ baking pan, and bake in the middle of a preheated oven for about 40 minutes. Let the cake cool in the pan before turning out.

Applesauce Cake

This is another example of a cake that is well-suited to an outdoor meal. Wrapped in foil, it stays moist and travels well. I think that it needs no frosting, but if you would like one, mix confectioner's sugar and lemon juice to make a thin glaze for it.

½ cup butter (1 stick), softened
1 cup sugar
1 egg
2 cups flour, sifted
½ teaspoon baking soda
½ teaspoon baking powder
½ teaspoon salt
1 teaspoon cinnamon
½ teaspoon allspice
½ teaspoon ground cloves
1 cup applesauce
½ cup raisins
½ cup walnuts, coarsely chopped

Preheat oven to 350 degrees.

Cream softened butter with sugar in a big mixing bowl. Add egg, stirring well. Sift flour with baking soda, baking powder, salt and spices. Stir flour into butter mixture. Add applesauce. Finally, stir in walnuts and raisins. Pour into a well-buttered loaf pan (approximately 9″×5″), and bake for 55 minutes. Allow to cool in pan before turning out.

Carrot Cake

1½ cups flour, sifted
¼ teaspoon allspice
⅛ teaspoon nutmeg
1 teaspoon cinnamon
1 teaspoon baking powder
1 teaspoon baking soda
½ cup white sugar
½ cup brown sugar, lightly-
  packed
½ cup butter, softened
2 eggs
1 teaspoon vanilla
1 teaspoon grated lemon or
  orange rind
1½ cups grated carrots
½ cup walnuts or pecans,
  coarsely chopped

Preheat oven to 375 degrees.

Sift together flour, baking powder, baking soda, cinnamon, nutmeg and allspice. Cream together butter and sugar. Beat in eggs. Add flour gradually, stirring constantly. Add vanilla, lemon or orange rind, carrots and nuts. Bake in a buttered 9″×5″ loaf pan for 55 minutes, until a knife comes out clean. Let cool in the pan on a rack before turning out. This keeps well wrapped in a double layer of foil.

Classic Brownies

An American picnic hardly seems complete without a healthy supply of chocolate brownies, well-laden with walnuts. This recipe produces a light, cake-like brownie.

3 ounces unsweetened chocolate
½ cup butter
1 cup sugar
2 eggs
½ cup flour, sifted
½ teaspoon baking powder
½ teaspoon salt
1 teaspoon vanilla
1 cup walnuts, chopped coarsely

Preheat oven to 350 degrees.

Melt chocolate over low heat. Cream the softened butter and sugar together in a bowl. Stir in the two eggs, lightly beaten, and the chocolate. Gradually add the flour, salt and baking powder, combining everything well. Stir in vanilla and walnuts. Pour the dough into a buttered baking pan about nine inches square. Bake for 30 minutes and allow to cool before cutting into squares. Brownies can be served right from the pan or wrapped individually in foil or plastic wrap.

Not-So-Classic Brownies

The recipe above is a familiar one. The following variation on the brownie theme is quite different, resulting in a chewier, fudgier two-tone brownie. Some people like one, some people prefer the other. Fortunately, they're both a cinch to make.

1 cup butter, softened
1 cup brown sugar, loosely-packed
1 cup white sugar
2 eggs
1 cup flour, sifted
½ teaspoon salt
3 teaspoons baking powder
1 teaspoon vanilla
1 cup walnuts or pecans, coarsely-chopped
1 cup chocolate bits

Preheat oven to 350 degrees. Cream together butter and sugar in a mixing bowl. Beat in the eggs, followed by the flour, salt and baking powder. Stir in the vanilla and walnuts. Spread the dough in a buttered 9″×12″ baking pan, and scatter the chocolate bits on top. Bake for about 35 minutes, and allow to cool before cutting into squares.

Oatmeal Cookies

These cookies are both crisp and chewy. They are not fragile, so they're perfect candidates for a picnic basket.

½ cup brown sugar, firmly packed
½ cup white sugar
½ cup butter, softened
1 egg
1 scant cup flour, sifted
½ teaspoon baking soda
½ teaspoon baking powder
½ teaspoon salt
1 teaspoon vanilla
1 cup uncooked oats, preferably the slow-cooking kind
½ cup raisins

Preheat oven to 350 degrees.

Cream softened butter and sugars together. Beat in egg. Gradually add flour, baking soda, baking powder, salt and vanilla, beating until smooth. Stir in oats and raisins. Drop teaspoonfuls of dough about two inches apart on a buttered cookie sheet. Bake for about ten minutes, until the cookies are lightly browned. Remove the cookies with a spatula and cool them on a rack. Makes about three dozen.

Shortbread

Shortbread is an ideal picnic dessert: it can be made ahead of time, is easy to transport and is rich and delicious without taking up a lot of space. An English friend gave me this recipe, with the unusual touch of fine semolina to give the finished shortbread a slight crunch.

2 cups butter, softened, plus 1 tablespoon
1 cup sugar
3 cups flour
½ cup fine semolina

Preheat oven to 350 degrees.

With an electric hand mixer or a large wooden spoon, cream together butter and sugar. Gradually add flour and semolina, mixing together well. You will end up with a dry dough. Grease a 9″ brownie pan with 1 tablespoon butter. Press dough firmly into the pan, and bake for about 25 minutes, until the shortbread is lightly-colored and slightly browned around the edges. Remove from oven, and prick the top in a decorative pattern with a fork. Allow to cool in the pan. Shortbread, well-wrapped in foil, will keep for several days in the refrigerator.

Fruit Salad

Cut-up fruit, marinating in its own juices, remains the best of desserts and seems especially appropriate to summer picnics, whether it is served out of crystal bowls or in paper cups.

Its character depends on the fruits available at the moment, but most fruit salads start out with one or more citrus fruits peeled and sectioned over the bowl, so that the juices aren't wasted. Firm fruits such as apples and grapes can be added next, and the citrus juices will keep them from turning brown. Soft fruits such as bananas and strawberries should be added as close as possible to serving time. You will probably not need sugar, but if you decide you do, make a simple sugar syrup by heating equal amounts of sugar and water until the sugar dissolves. A little Kirsch also can be added to perk up the flavor of a fruit salad.

The following recipe is an example of a simple, summery fruit salad.

2 oranges
1 lemon
2 apples, cut into thin slices
1 cup seedless grapes
2 bananas
2 peaches, peeled and cut into
    eighths
1 cup strawberries
1 tablespoon fresh mint, chopped
    fine

Cut away peel and pith of oranges, and, using a small, sharp knife, push sections of fruit away from the membrane, dropping them into a bowl and making sure that all the juice also goes into the bowl. Add the juice of the lemon. Add apple slices, grapes, peaches, cut-up bananas and strawberries, keeping in mind that soft fruits should be put in close to serving time. Gently stir in mint. In a few minutes taste to see if sugar syrup is necessary.

Figs with Madeira

This is a festive way to serve the ripe figs of summer. It is especially pretty if you can find both deep purple and pale green figs, but it can be done successfully with either. Be sure to select figs that are ripe but not disintegrating, so that they will keep their shape when stirred. Serve them in a shallow bowl, adding the cream at the last moment. Whipped cream can be transported in a Thermos bottle.

2 pounds figs
¾ cup Madeira
1 cup heavy cream
¼ cup sugar

Slice off the pointed ends of the figs, and cut each fig into quarters vertically. Place them in a bowl and pour ½ cup Madeira over them. Stir gently and chill in the refrigerator for at least two hours. Whip cream until it forms soft points, stir in sugar and remaining Madeira. Just before serving, pour cream over figs.

65

INDEX

NOTES

NOTES

OTHER BOOKS BY
TAYLOR & NG PRESS

WOKCRAFT by Charles & Violet Schafer. An authoritative and entertaining book on the art of Chinese wok cookery. Authentic, easy-to-follow recipes for beginners and professionals alike. Illustrated by Win Ng.

RICECRAFT: Margaret Gin delves into the fact, fiction and fancy of rice. A collection of inventive recipes, from simple to exotic, takes full advantage of the international versitility of rice. Fanciful illustrations by Win Ng.

TEACRAFT: Charles and Violet Schafer's tea treasury of romance, rituals & recipes explores tea's origin, its extensive variety and multiplicity of uses. A test and taste chapter guides you to a true connoisseurship. Illustrated by Win Ng.

HERBCRAFT: Violet Schafer unveils the mysteries, origins, history, growing and storing conditions of 26 herbs in a delightful Win Ng illustrated handbook. *Herbcraft* also charts gardens and records healthful recipes.

COFFEE: The story behind your morning cup—exploring the history and lore of coffee, grinding and brewing hints, what to brew it in, etc. Charles and Violet Schafer also cite a delicious collection of companion food recipes. Photo-illustrated.

CHINESE VILLAGE COOKBOOK: Celebrated Rhoda Yee tells you all about the wok and Chinese cookery, with colorful narratives on everyday life in a Chinese village, excellent easy to prepare recipes and a helpful stirfrying chart.

DIM SUM: Rhoda Yee's second book reveals the savory secrets of Dim Sum, the traditional Chinese tea lunch and helps you prepare it in your home. Techniques and end results are photo-documented.

GREAT ASIA STEAMBOOK: Irene Wong's practical guide to steam cooking techniques and recipes from all Asian countries. A delicious blending of an international cuisine that is both nutritious and energy-saving. Photo-illustrated.

NO PRESSURE STEAM COOKING: Robert Zinkhon's delightful guide to a wide range of steamed foods from meats to vegetables, breads to desserts. Steam cooking's energy-saving & nutritional qualities are matched with time-saving techniques.

DOG & CAT GOOD FOOD BOOK: Author Terri McGinnis, veterinarian and pet expert, unravels the myths about what foods are nutritionally beneficial to pets of all ages; lists charts to guide and recipes that work. Illustrated by Margaret Choi.